After the Leaves Fall

AFTER THE LEAVES
Fall

A Winter in the Northwoods

Jack Becklund

NORTH STAR PRESS OF ST. CLOUD, INC.

Library of Congress Cataloging-in-Publication Data

Becklund, Jack.
    After the leaves fall : a winter in the Northwoods /
    Jack Becklund.
        p. cm.
    ISBN 0-87839-166-5 (alk. paper)
        1. Forest animals—Minnesota—Anecdotes.
        2. Winter—Minnesota—Anecdotes. I. Title.

QL185 .B43 2001
591.73'09776--dc21   2001044152

Photos by Patti and Jack Becklund

Copyright © 2001 Jack Becklund

First Edition July 2001

ISBN: 0-87839-166-5

Printed in the United States of America by Versa Press,
Inc., East Peoria, Illinois.

Published by
North Star Press of St. Cloud, Inc.
P.O. Box 451
St. Cloud, Minnesota 56302

*This book is dedicated to
my father,
who instilled in me a love for the Northwoods,
and to
my mother,
who taught me the power of the written word.*

❄ Table of Contents ❄

After the Leaves Fall

Elbow Creek behind our house—just before the leaves fell.

1

❄ Ready or Not ❄

Amazing. Just the first week of October, the start of fall, and most of the birch and aspen leaves already carpeted the forest floor. The cold rain spattering against my windshield would soon finish ripping the leaves from the trees and turn the crisp, golden ground cover to a dull, sodden brown.

I had forgotten how fast all this could happen. Two weeks before, leaf lookers clogged back roads. Scenic Pine Mountain Road and South Brule Road became so dusty from the traffic that partridge hunters went elsewhere. But there was no escaping the leaf crowd. They discovered every pair of ruts that led to a pile of sawdust in the forest. So the hunters, locals mostly, waited until the leaves fell, and the flatlanders went home, and the cash registers fell silent. About now.

I pulled into the station to get gas and minnows, and Butch Schulte spotted my Florida plates.

"Gonna be winter soon," he warned with a grin, wondering why we hadn't yet headed south.

"I've spent thirty-five winters in northern Minnesota. Figure one more won't hurt me."

"Really? Got enough anti-freeze?"

"You bet," I answered quickly without really knowing if I did. *I'll have it tested*, I thought, remembering the painful cost of an earlier cracked radiator.

Butch looked up at the high ridge that rose fifteen hundred feet above Lake Superior. "You just come down the trail?"

"Yup."

"Could get some snow up there tonight," he said, adding another quick grin for emphasis.

"A little early, isn't it?" I said doubtfully.

"Maybe. Never can tell. Feels like snow." He smiled and put my twenty into the register. "If you're staying here, you'll need to have a look at my snowmobiles, over at the shop."

"Yeah, I saw your sign over there. I'll stop by."

He nodded with another smile as I took my plastic bag of minnows out into the rain.

Three miles up the hill, near the ridge locals call Sawtooth Mountain, I drove the Jeep into Butch's prophecy. At first the raindrops got bigger, heavier, as if they were making a statement before running down the windshield. Then they stopped running altogether, sort of stuck to the glass. You could see it in the air ahead, a haze that took on whiteness as it dimmed the visibility. Snow.

A big log truck emerged from the flakes near the ridge, geared down and slowed to no more than twenty on the grade. Wet snow plastered his windshield where the wipers missed.

I smiled with genuine feeling. Back home after fifteen years in Florida. Living in the woods I had loved as a boy. Hunkering down for a winter in the north country. I could hardly wait to get home, another three miles up the Gunflint Trail, and share the first snowfall, however fleeting, with my wife, Patti.

Our place in the woods was set back a quarter mile from the main road and overlooked Elbow Creek. Two A-frames that were house, garage, and storage. We called it the "house of a thousand nooks and crannies." That may have been an understatement.

The snow melted as it fell on the gravel driveway, but the grass was frosted white as I pulled up to the house. Patti and our black lab, Ramah, came out to greet me.

"You should have been here" she gushed. "It was really coming down. I could hardly see."

"So you think you're ready for a real Minnesota winter?" I asked.

"Oh, yes," she said quietly, "I love it here."

The dog, snuffling in the snowy grass for something unseen, popped her head up with a white fluff on her nose and wagged her tail.

"Looks like she's ready, too," Patti laughed.

"Guess we'd better get serious, then, and start up the heating system," I said. "Soon it'll be too cold for just the fireplace."

Patti looked at me seriously. The heating system was complex, possibly even dangerous, and we both were nervous about it.

"Promise you'll get someone to help," she urged.

"Tomorrow morning, first thing, I'll call Phil Hedstrom."

✳ ✳ ✳

The thing I noticed about Phil Hedstrom's blue pickup truck, once I got past the grime that quickly accumulated from driving on dirt and mud roads, was that the license plates were three years old. I shrugged and guessed it didn't matter much if you stayed off the main highway that ran along the north shore of Lake Superior.

A retired logger and lumberman, Phil stood six-foot-two even hunched over a bit. His hair was thinning, what I called wispy, and, when he spoke, I'd swear there was a melody just under the surface. His watery blue eyes had a sparkle when he liked you.

Phil was the resident expert on this type of heating system, which featured a wood-chip burner, a boiler, a storage tank, an automatic fuel-feeder system, six zones, and about a thousand feet of copper piping. All this, well most of this, I could figure out. What baffled me was the dozens of valves placed with diabolical care that needed to be turned in just the right combination for the cold water to be heated and then returned to warm the house. Alone, I could more likely pick the lock on a bank vault.

"Well, it's not so very hard, once you get the hang of it," Phil explained, drawing on the cigarette stuck to his lips. "Just give me a minute to remember what's what."

We were standing in a specially built room beneath the garage. This was where the cold water came to be heated. Above us was the fuel supply, a roomful of wood chips. We filled the room by shoveling chips from a semi-trailer outside the garage onto a conveyor belt. At the end of the belt, the chips fell into the room. In the chip room was another conveyor that transported the chips to a vertical shaft that fed the furnace below. This was activated by an electric eye.

I swear I am trying to simplify this as I go. There were actually more things going on with the system. The operation had a Rube Goldberg quality that made me suspect a mouse on a treadmill behind it all.

But Phil, bless him, was up to the task. His son had owned the house, and Phil had often been in charge of the heat plant, as he was now.

"Okay, stick the newspaper in there. Light it," he said.

I take instruction well in certain matters, especially when fear is involved. I lit the crumpled newspaper page and stepped back, doubtful but expectant.

"Now what?" I asked.

"We wait 'til she catches."

We hovered over the small furnace from our two folding chairs and watched the flicker of flames through the grated door.

For a couple of minutes, nothing much happened. Then a sputtering noise began, increasing in intensity until it steadied into the roar of a jet engine.

"Jeez," I shouted. "It isn't going to explode, is it?"

He shook his head. "She really burns good, though, eh?"

"Whoa, I guess so. Now what?"

"Now we settle back and make sure the feeder's working. That's about it."

We settled, hiking our chairs back against the wall and lighting up cigarettes. I was reminded of the day in sixth grade when I had to get a school janitor out of the boiler room. Right now, I suspected, we looked just like a couple of janitors hanging out in the boiler room.

After a few minutes, Phil checked the boiler gauges and sent a flow of hot water toward the five-hundred-gallon storage tank in the basement. As for the chip feeder system, he was more cautious.

"Check every couple of hours to make sure it's not hung up," he suggested.

"What could happen?" I asked.

He shrugged, "Might go out." Then he hesitated a few seconds before adding, "or it could try to burn up the feeder tube."

"You mean this thing leading up to the chip storage room?" I asked, growing fearful again.

"It probably won't, but just check it every so often, and you won't have any problem."

I know he was trying to make it sound simple and safe, but I was not reassured. Throughout the winter, I was never away from that jet fighter of a furnace for more than two hours at a time. At night, and whenever we left for longer periods, the chip burner was shut down.

A couple of weeks later, I felt vindicated in my caution. Dick Gilbertson, a Norwegian bachelor we'd met at church, stopped by to pick up a casserole. When he climbed down from his pickup, he stopped a moment in thought. "You know," he said, "I've been in here before. I think it was with the Maple Hill Fire Department."

This is the kind of news that can make cheeks tingle, even on a cold day. "You mean, like a fire call?"

He nodded his head, "Yeah, but I can't remember what it was. Chimney fire maybe?"

After that, my attention to all things that burned around the house—trash barrel, fireplace, chip burner, potbellied stove—was even more resolute.

*　*　*

In the back country, birch and maple aren't just for esthetics; they are the fuel that provides low-priced heat through the long winter. The wood is cut to eight foot lengths, and a stack four feet wide and four feet high equals a cord. When you burn wood, everything is measured by cords. An easy winter might require six cords, while something more severe could be called an "eight-cord winter."

It's easier to talk of cords than to get them cut and split. This is hot, hard and dangerous work. First comes the chain

Chipmunk storing up for the winter.

saw to cut long logs into stove lengths of fourteen or eighteen inches. Then, you bring out the axe, maul, and splitting wedge. This is shoulder- and back-building work, and, in early fall, you can hear the thump of an axe, its steel glistening from wear, as it splits the wood into halves and quarters. Or, you'll hear the ring of maul upon wedge, steel on steel, as it clears a stubborn knot.

The pile of split logs grows slowly; a hard day's work may yield no more than a cord of wood, a pair of blistered hands, and a number of sore muscles. A week's vacation spent cutting and splitting wood for the winter? It's not uncommon in a place where seasoned wood means winter survival.

So the wood piles mount, and the nights grow frosty, and many animals feel the clock ticking as they near hibernation. These are truly borrowed days for bears, raccoons, skunks, and chipmunks. Strange bears pass through, traveling far to satisfy a desperate hunger for food before they den between September 15th and October 1st. A skunk, Pepe Le Pew we call him, takes up residence on our back porch and dares the bears to stray close. In return, he offers a noseful of his unique perfume.

2

❄ Wild Neighbors ❄

At noon, we sat outside at the wrought iron table and chairs, enjoying a sandwich in the brief warmth. Frost had killed the usually pesky bugs, and we were free to enjoy the special sights and smells that are distinctly fall.

Along the rail, blue jays and chickadees gathered for sunflower seeds. Year-round residents, they had returned from raising babies and replaced the departed goldfinches, sparrows, and blackbirds that accepted our hospitality in summer.

Underfoot, the ever-present chipmunks careened like bumper cars in their competition for food. There was enough for everyone, but the little ground squirrels are combative even in the midst of plenty. A couple of the more courageous, or perhaps more stupid, of the chipmunk clan, scaled the chairs and discovered the bowl of almonds, unsalted and shelled, that we put on the table top. One we called Chester, easy to distinguish by his half tail and scar-laced back, managed to store eight in his cheeks before making a delivery run to his underground home.

Chester and his friend, who we called the Shy One, kept running nuts back to the folks at home, alternating arrival times on the table so they never ran suddenly nose to nose in the almond bowl. Patti pulled the bowl closer, so that it

was within our reach, and she actually touched the tiny creatures as they reloaded for each delivery. Chester felt her
light touch upon his back and shivered. Afraid, but unwilling to leave because the finger on his fur put him in a sort of
a trance, he endured a brief pet, then returned to the bowl
of plenty to finish filling his half-empty cheeks.

A staccato, high-pitched chatter interrupted the quiet of
the lazy day. Blue jays flew up, calling their warnings. Other
birds flew from the rail to the trees, where they had protection. The chatter was repeated, and we realized it was the
call of a red squirrel, a female we called Bertha. We thought
of her as "queen of the deck."

When we first arrived at our house, all the red squirrels
showed nervousness and fear. They'd chatter and flee when
we opened the door. As we put out sunflower seeds, they came
to understand we were not trying to hurt them, but most continued to keep their distance when we were outside.

Bertha, up on the railing, greets her huge cousin, the fox squirrel.

And then one squirrel began to stand out. She was not only unafraid, she also decided somehow that her assignment was to keep the other squirrels off the deck. We'd seen a dog decide that it's his job to guard the house, but a red squirrel? Yet that is what Bertha did. She would literally clear the deck of any competitors, chipmunks included, who dared trespass on her property. Sometimes, she would send them scurrying in a few minutes. Other times, it might take a hour; a couple of other red squirrels merited special attention, and she might chase them up and down through the birch and aspen until the two had raced out of sight. Chipmunks were hardly a challenge. She would brush them aside and drive the more stubborn ones right off the deck. We often thought the ten-foot fall would surely kill the frail little creatures, but no matter how they landed, they picked themselves up, gave a shake and went on their way.

As we sat in the sunlight listening to the murmur of the river and the whisper of tiny chipmunk feet, Bertha Squirrel was again on her way.

"Bertha," Patti called, watching her fast-moving squirrel friend outlined against the white of a large birch. "Come on, Bertha." "Here she comes," she added quietly to Chester's friend, who was stuffing another nut into his cheeks. "Better head for home." She gave a little push with her finger, and the startled chipmunk jumped across the table and shinnied down the chair. "Scoot," she added with a dismissing wave, and the chipmunk crossed the deck with his half-load of almonds.

And then Bertha was on the deck, chasing chipmunks. Two got away down the stairs, and a third flew off into space. There were no other squirrels that day, so her job was easy. Soon she was up on the table eyeing the nuts and wondering what sort of a treat they might be.

Patti took a nut in her fingers and held it out. The squirrel approached in nervous little jumps, then inched forward and gently took the almond in her paws. She sat up and

Chester the chipmunk in the nut basket.

turned the nut this way and that, trying to understand exactly what she had. Then she ran for the forest. She was back in
a couple of minutes for another.

"Just one at a time," I said. "Chester manages a half-
dozen or more. No wonder chipmunks can store up enough
for the winter, while squirrels only have food for a couple of
days. The squirrel has to hunt all winter."

Also, I thought, the squirrel often hides her nuts in the
spur of the moment. Places, like the crotch of a tree, where
they're easily stolen. Other times, she picks an obscure
place like the inside of a boot liner in the garage where I'd
discovered a half-dozen nuts that she had obviously for-

gotten. Overall, a somewhat haphazard food-storage system.

To compensate for her shortcomings, Bertha had energy to burn. She would run nuts, placing them in two or three different places, as long as we cared to sit out and give them to her. After a while though, Patti and I had other things to do.

"Okay, we'll leave you a small pile," Patti said to the squirrel.

After going inside, I looked back out to discover that the squirrel's nuts had been discovered and were fast disappearing. The sharp-eyed blue jays had spied them and were carrying off a few whenever Bertha left on a delivery run. Undaunted, when the almonds were gone, she simply hunkered down to eat sunflowers seeds.

Late that afternoon, I'd arranged to go walleye fishing with a young fellow I had met. I'd supply boat, motor, and bait; he'd bring his local knowledge of Cascade Lake. We got to the landing with a couple of hours of daylight remaining and launched the fourteen-foot aluminum boat. After trying one place, then another without much success, we found ourselves in a small bay at the west end. The sun was sliding behind the spruce and pines when we first heard the call.

"Wolves?" I asked.

He nodded, listening as first one wolf, then another, and a third laced their mournful cries into a haunting chorus. In the still of the evening, their song echoed across the water.

I had heard wolves several times at night as I sat outside on our back deck but never this close, never while I was out in the woods away from home. We were alone, the only boat on the lake.

I don't know what possessed me, but I quietly said, "I'm gonna try calling back," and gave my best rendition of a falsetto howl.

When first one, then a second wolf howled in response, the hair on my neck shot straight out. I howled again, and my fishing partner chimed in. This time, several wolves joined the chorus. It sounded as though they were coming closer.

We looked at each other in disbelief, and I shook my head. One or two wolves continued to howl, but the rest of the pack was coming our way. We could hear them breaking twigs and making an occasional yip. Now I was truly grateful we were in a boat a hundred feet from shore.

Soon we saw lighter shapes moving through the dark underbrush, hugging the shoreline. And then, in an opening, a big gray timber wolf stepped out and looked at us. He was joined by two or three smaller wolves. Then another adult, then a couple more of the junior variety. Soon, three adults and five nearly grown pups stood panting, drinking cold lake water and eyeing us.

The pups soon lost interest, and two began to play. Other wolves were passing through the brush behind them without stepping out. Only two of the adults stood and stared silently.

And then they turned and were gone. We could hear them moving through the forest, a pack of a dozen or more timber wolves on the move. I howled once more, and one wolf answered, as if for old times' sake, then they were gone.

"Whoa," I said, sitting back and relaxing as the blue sky darkened to purple. "That was something."

Ten years earlier, after years of being hunted and trapped, the timber wolves of Minnesota numbered only a few hundred. They were designated a protected animal, and slowly, steadily, their numbers increased. The count in 1988 stood at about 1,200.

Despite catching no walleyes that evening, it was a memorable fishing trip. Incredibly, another encounter followed just a month later.

This time, Patti and I were driving north on the Gunflint Trail about two miles north of our house. We could see the Gunflint Pines, a stand of old-growth white pines, up ahead.

In the distance, something dark, two dark objects actually, crossed the road.

"What are they?" I asked.

Patti, who has the good eyes for distance work, said, "I know this sounds crazy, but they look like wolves."

It had snowed the night before, maybe four or five inches, and the white ground made a good contrast. We noted up ahead where the animals had gone off the road into the woods. Just past the spot, an old logging road was still passable and led out into a cutover filled with buggy-whip aspens. We'd been on it before, and I knew the Jeep could handle it.

"Hang on. I'm going off through that opening," I said as we passed the wolves' saucer-size prints in the snow. "Maybe we'll get another glimpse."

I knew it was a long shot, but I turned and went careening down through the woods, snow flying. We emerged in the old clearing, and I stopped suddenly. Not more than a hundred feet away, a beautiful gray-mottled wolf stood silently, eyes appraising us. We sat staring at each other for maybe ten seconds, then he set out at a lope through the dense screen of aspen and was soon gone.

"Wow." It was about all I could say.

Patti was more lucid. "What a beautiful animal. Did you see the way he looked at us? Very cool and intelligent."

"Hold on a second," I said. "I'm going down there and have a look at his tracks." I opened the door and started through the snow. Suddenly, there was movement ahead as a second wolf, unseen until now, trotted along the same trail.

This wolf was almost coal-black with light eyes, a bit smaller than the first, I thought probably a female. She was no more than seventy-five feet away as I stood there, watching her go. When she was a hundred yards past me, she joined her mate in a quick glance back, then they were gone.

I walked down and looked at their prints in the snow, easily four or five inches across, and thought of the wild creatures that had left them just moments earlier. How lucky we had been to see this pair so closely. Few people, even those who live in the area, ever see so many wolves in such a short time, let alone anytime.

※ ※ ※

In Cook County, frost and Labor Day are synonymous. If the corn in the garden hasn't ripened by then, it is probably out of luck.

By mid-September, all those beautiful garden plants that once sprouted green and bore vegetables are dark, wilted and dead.

The garden appears to be a wasteland. But this is where the Cook County surprise comes in, for, beneath the ground, still protected from the gathering cold, the root crops wait to be unearthed. Locals have learned that these vegetables— potatoes, rutabagas, carrots, beets, onions—develop a bit more character and better skins if left for a while after the first September frost.

Our garden, which had been rated "not so hot" by the previous owners, still contained a random crop of rogue potatoes, spread here and there. I should have marked the leafy tops before they fell over and died, because by the time I'd brought a garden fork and stirred myself to dig, it was almost impossible to know where to do it. So I dug here and dug there. I found hundreds of nice-sized rocks, many of which at first looked like potatoes. Ultimately I collected a medium-sized berry bucket nearly full of the genuine article.

There was a rusty old Rototiller sitting behind the shed, overgrown with vines and bushes. It was a hand-me-down left behind by the previous owners, and, as the leaves fell, its presence was revealed. Following the great potato harvest, I hauled it out, checked gas and plugs and gave it a few pulls. It roared into life, and, in a rare moment of ambition,

I tilled the entire garden and threw many more rocks into the woods.

I was very excited about having a garden the following spring, but by then, a new crop of rocks seemed to have grown in the soil, and the old tiller had coughed and wheezed its last and refused ever again to start.

Mostly, commencing that fall, the garden area became a playground for the animals. As autumn deepened, a number of deer gathered in the evenings to eat grass and romp around. One of them was a majestic buck with a heavy, eight-point rack of antlers. A second, smaller buck was his ever-present companion. We called them Big Buck and Little Buck, respectively. The other deer were does, fawns, and yearlings. They were all respectful and wary when the two bucks were around.

At first, when Patti or I went outside, the deer would run away. Soon, however, if we were going to the garage or clothesline, they would stand and watch.

I found out where to buy whole corn by the hundred-pound sack, so I thought we'd give the deer a treat. The two bucks started making regular appearances at the corn pile. We moved the corn a little closer. We sat outside to watch them, and, although they seemed nervous, they stayed. Finally, I discovered I could carry a small bucket of corn out to the pile while Little Buck stood nearby watching. As long as I didn't make eye contact—just kept looking down as I walked—he would remain. I suppose I got within ten feet of the young forkhorn that fall.

Most people think of deer as gentle, soft-eyed creatures, but one only has to observe awhile to learn they are some-times mean and cantankerous. The bucks would chase the does from the corn, and the large does would chase other does and yearlings so their own fawns could eat first. A fixed pecking order developed, and woe unto the poor deer that forgot it. He or she might get an antler butt or hoof slash for the violation.

When we put out the corn in October, we got an almost immediate bonus. A flock of ducks were soon circling overhead and seemed to understand there was something to eat down there. They set their wings after three loops above the tree line and appeared ready to settle onto the lawn near the corn, only to flare away at the last second. However, a few of the bold ones did land and were soon eating the corn. Seeing their friends safe and well-fed brought several more spiraling in, but most of the flock went on.

We counted nine mallards at or near the corn pile that day, and next morning when we glanced out, there appeared to be five. *But wait, aren't those ducks different from yesterday's flock?* These were wood ducks, perhaps the most beautiful ducks in the world and not uncommon in northern Minnesota with its dense woods and many ponds. In fact,

The deer we called Big Buck.

while fishing on several area lakes, we had seen a number of wood duck nesting boxes placed by the state Department of Natural Resources to foster wood duck reproduction.

The mallards returned, and the wood ducks stayed on, and this began what we called the Great Duck War. The mallards held the upper hand in size and numbers, but the wood ducks proved tenacious and determined. Each group claimed a section of the yard as its own, and all the ducks respected this division, but when either group made a move toward the corn, war would erupt. Whenever a couple of wood ducks strode toward the corn pile, a half-dozen mallard interceptors would move in on them. Sometimes they succeeded; other times their appearance would simply cause the wood ducks to rally in support, which would aggravate the rest of the mallards. Soon, all the ducks were fully involved, chasing and pecking at each other's tails.

We never tired of watching the various strategies used to gain control of the food. The mallards came straight ahead, while the faster woodies circled to draw off their enemies, then dashed for the food.

After several hours of such antics, both sides would fly down to Elbow Creek behind the house where the mallards claimed a pond area, and the wood ducks took up station on the rocks downstream. Once again, peace would prevail across our land.

3

❄ Moose on the Loose ❄

After fifteen years in Florida, the cold came on faster, more intensely, than we expected. A day of almost summer-like warmth, complete with bees droning and that unmistakable smell of fall was followed by a hard overnight freeze and, the next morning, a cold, cutting wind out of the north. We had planned to go brook trout fishing on a nearby lake but scratched the idea. I even took the canoe off the top of the Jeep as a flock of Canadian geese honking overhead, urged us to follow their migration.

"Maybe I should be organizing the garage for winter," I said, warming my backside near the crackling fireplace.

Ever the diplomat, Patti said, "Only if you feel like it. You were also going to put insulation against those cold concrete walls in the basement and, if I'm not mistaken, that weedy field we call a lawn needs one last mowing."

"No shortage to choose from," I responded thoughtfully. "If I don't mow now, the grass will be covered with snow, and if I don't insulate the basement, we'll be cold down there. Interesting choice."

"Maybe that's why everybody else was getting ready for winter last month," Patti teased.

"Tell you what," I said, the decision made, "I'll play catch-up all day tomorrow, work like a beaver, but today let's hit a couple of those real remote logging roads and see what's out there now that the leaves have gone and the visibility's better. Maybe we'll even see a moose."

"Don't say that. Whenever you predict something, it doesn't happen."

"The only way we'll find out is by getting out there," I shrugged.

During the summer, we had discovered that several old logging roads, overgrown but still passable, led five or six miles off the main road if one knew which turns to make. These seldom-used roads also led, at times, to unknown creeks and beaver ponds containing big brook trout.

One day, south of the Greenwood Road, we'd worked our way up to a small beaver pond that on first cast yielded a thirteen-inch trout. Another spot on that same rutted and rock-strewn road contained the mother lode of blueberries that we managed to spot hidden behind a screen of hazel brush. Fortunately, we beat most of the bears to that quarter acre of berries and filled our buckets with the blue treasures.

But now, the stark sepia-tone landscape offered vistas not apparent to the summer traveler. And that day, despite my prediction, we really did see a moose. Actually, two moose. A cow and her half-grown calf. It was a confrontation we will not soon forget.

They came up out of a dense clump of bushes in tandem, then saw us in the Jeep and halted in the middle of the road. So did we. That cow was not only huge, she looked like she'd been in the gym lifting weights. And she had that look in her eye that said, "I could crush you if I want, and I think I might want to do it." If there ever was a moose with an attitude, this was the one.

"Will she charge?" Patti asked, reading my thoughts.

"I don't know, but I'm gonna give her some more room." I replied tensely and shifted into reverse. I backed about fifty feet down the road, glancing between the rear-view mirror and the moose's massive presence in front of us. She took two or three steps toward us, then stopped. We waited. She waited, never taking her eyes off us.

By backing up, we had doubled the distance between us, but this was one large and frightening moose ready, and certainly able, to protect her calf. With a shoulder height of seven feet and a weight of eight or nine hundred pounds, she feared no other creature in the woods.

We waited, tension crackling, for more than five minutes. During that time, her eyes never left us. Then finally, she glanced away and within a few seconds crossed the road and moved through the thick brush with her calf at her hip.

Driving home, we talked about the strange inclinations of the moose. Just a week earlier, we were returning home at night down the Gunflint Trail when a large bull ran out in front of us. I slowed, and the moose trotted ahead of us down the road. He moved to the side as if to let us pass, but when we attempted to go by, he speeded up and moved out in front of us. We went down the darkened road like this, almost but not quite able to pass him, for almost a mile. Finally, nearing the Trout Lake Road, car headlights appeared coming our way. I slowed, not knowing what that crazy moose might do, and started flashing my high beams on and off to warn the other driver. Luckily, as the cars came together, Mr. Moose casually trotted off into the woods.

The peak of moose rut, or mating season, occurs in early October. For several weeks in the fall, they are aggressive and unpredictable. My grandfather used to tell the story of his duck hunt, which occurred one evening a few miles north of Grand Marais.

"There were ducks quacking in the pond," he would explain in his thick Swedish accent. "So we lit birch bark torches to see them better. Just then, we heard something coming through the woods. It was the moose. Everyone ran away, but the moose, he picks me to go after. So I climbed this tree and waited, but the moose, he didn't want to leave. He even tried to push the tree down. In the morning, I climbed down, but the moose, he was waiting, and I had to climb back up in the tree. Then after a while, he left again, and this time, I climbed down and got my gun and sneaked away. Everybody else had gone, and I had to walk all the way home."

This story was a regular after-dinner entertainment during my boyhood years, and I still remember how Grandfather's animated gestures and twinkling eyes added to the telling. After learning the story by heart, I was much influenced by it and fully expected a moose to appear at any moment to chase me up a tree.

Fortunately, it never happened, but it wasn't a far-fetched idea, and it did happen to others over the years.

That night, after dinner, we heard a squabble erupt on the back porch. The last bear had left to hibernate three weeks earlier, so we had no idea what it might be. We turned on the overhead deck light, and there, on the deck railing, was a trio of young raccoons. We'd heard raccoons arguing once up by the garden several weeks earlier, but now they appeared in person. Patti ran for the camera, and we shot photos.

As we watched them, the young raccoons suddenly stopped eating sunflower seeds and stared over into the darkness near the stairs. Soon they were whimpering, looking around for an escape route, and even urinating on the bench in fear. Something was terrifying them, but what could it be?

The answer was soon made known as the biggest boar coon I've ever seen came out of the dark.

"I didn't know they got so big," Patti exclaimed in awe. The animal looked as big as our yearling bear cubs.

I just shook my head and watched the deck explode into action as young raccoons fled every which way from the growling, menacing he-coon. Soon all was calm, and the big fellow settled down for a snack of seeds.

But his enjoyment was short-lived as Patti opened the sliding glass door and scolded him for chasing off the youngsters. He cut his meal short and went skulking off into the night.

Next morning, I included the raccoons in the column I was writing for the local newspaper. A couple of old-time readers read about the raccoons and declared I must have been seeing things, since there were no raccoons in Cook County. Fortunately, we had good photos of the raccoons, and a number of residents chimed in with their own raccoon stories to provide irrefutable evidence of their existence in the area.

We never saw the big raccoon again, but as luck would have it, we would be seeing more of the young raccoons, and their adventures around Easter time.

* * *

I had last hunted deer in the area thirty years earlier, and much had changed in that time. Meadows were now forests, and big forests were cut-over scrub. A couple of weeks before the season opened, in early November, I decided it would be a good idea to have a close look at all the places I had hunted to see what had happened to them.

Our first outing took place on Sunday after returning from church, where we'd noticed more empty pews than usual.

"People are heading south," I said. "Summer people are gone, senior citizens are leaving to become snowbirds, and now that the leaf watchers are gone, the resorts and restaurant people are taking some time off before the winter season sets in."

We changed, grabbed a sandwich and loaded the car with our black lab, Ramah, and assorted gear. It was overcast and looked like snow. A flock of white buntings swirled ahead of us down the driveway. The grass still looked shamefully in need of mowing. I hoped the snow would cover it soon and wipe away my guilty conscience. I hated the idea of having to mow in near freezing weather with the second-hand machine I had bought when we arrived. It had cost me twenty-five dollars and worked no better than its price.

We traveled several miles west on the back roads, then turned off the Bally Creek Road into the logging road that led to my hunting spot. Parking after about a quarter mile, we unloaded the dog, and I loaded my shotgun in case any wayward partridge should wander our way.

We walked about half a mile through country that had grown up and changed a lot since I'd last been there. There were few tracks to be seen as Ramah worked back and forth, examining the many smells that all labs find interesting.

We were moving generally northwest into roadless country, when, suddenly, I heard the piercing call of first one, then three or four wolves carried toward us on the wind.

They were a long way off, probably more than half a mile, and I was certain they hadn't smelled or heard us, but the high-pitched howls sent a cold chill up my neck, and I motioned to Patti to stop.

Ramah heard them too, and, although she was a Florida dog and had never seen a wolf, she made a smart U-turn, as if to say, "Well, I think we've gone far enough, so I'll turn here and lead you guys back to the car."

When she went trotting past us toward the car, Patti and I erupted with laughter. It was truly funny to see the dog, trying to be brave, but really quite frightened, trying to encourage us, but never slowing down.

We got back to the car to find her halfway under it. She came out with tail wagging and led us to the back door where she hopped in happily and smothered us with dog kisses.

I saw few signs of deer that day and no partridge, but I had been diligently harvesting the birds on a number of outings and now had about two dozen in the garage freezer. So, on the way home, I suggested we bake up a couple for supper.

"I've never cooked them before, so I don't know anything about them," Patti said.

I volunteered to do the cooking and served up each of the partridge, or ruffed grouse as they're formally called.

It was soon apparent Patti was not eating her bird. "Don't you like it?" I asked.

"I'm sorry," she said, "but when I put a piece in my mouth and try to swallow it, my throat just closed. I can't do it."

"Percy Partridge?" I asked. During the summer, and now especially in the fall, we'd been adopted by a male partridge, whom Patti named Percy, and who now sat on the back deck eating seeds while dwarfing the other birds.

"I suppose that's it," she said sorrowfully, apologizing profusely.

I tried to reassure her that it was fine, while mentally I thought of people who would enjoy the birds I'd already provisioned. It was certain that partridge would no longer be served in our household.

❊ ❊ ❊

As if to punctuate our decision, the next morning, when we let out Caesar, our big outdoor male cat, he came around to the front door and immediately encountered Percy. We stood at the dining room window watching as the tableau unfolded.

First, they both stood their ground about twenty-five feet apart. Then slowly, steadily, Percy began to advance. Caesar didn't know what to make of this bold bird, so, at a distance of about ten feet, he broke and ran away to the backyard where he asked to be let into the safety of the house.

Until we left Florida, a few months earlier, Caesar lived outdoors where he survived cars, dogs, and other cats, in his life as a stray. After moving with us to the northwoods, he insisted on being outdoors each day. So far, it had worked out well, but with the colder weather and other predators on the prowl, we kept a closer eye on his daily outing.

Next morning, there was an inch or more snow on the back deck when he asked to go out.

"This will be interesting," Patti said, looking first at the snow, then at the cat.

Caesar stepped out gingerly into the strange substance, then raised a dainty paw and shook off the white stuff. He thought twice about going on, then looked back and saw us watching which shamed him into moving forward.

We kept an eye on him for an hour or so, as he traversed the snowy yard and went into the woods. Finally, he emerged

Percy Partridge in full regalia.

and started back toward us along the driveway, looking like a lost little hobo. We could tell he was cold just from the way he walked, all scrunched up. Then halfway down the driveway, about fifty yards from the house, he stopped suddenly. The reason was soon apparent as first Little Buck, then Big Buck, stepped out of the woods. They too, stopped as they saw the cat. We watched an interesting stand off with the adversaries about thirty or forty feet apart.

"I better get out there and shoo away the deer," Patti said quickly. "They could hurt Caesar."

"No, no, let's wait and see," I responded. "He knows enough to get up a tree if necessary."

We stood in the dining room and watched as the two deer and the little black cat stood watching each other. Finally, Little Buck lowered his head, stretched it toward the cat and cocked his ears. This was all it took to send the cat leaping toward the house. The deer watched but made no further move toward him. Soon he was at the back door, calling us to let him in.

"Well, then, big fellow," Patti said in a soothing voice. "We're glad to see you back safe and sound."

Caesar was apparently very glad to have escaped the "monsters." He became an indoor cat after that, and never again went outside in the nearly eight more years we lived on Elbow Creek.

❊ ❊ ❊

With snow on the ground and more starting to fall, I was at least spared the odious job of cutting the lawn. It was gone from sight until late April or early May, a six-month reprieve.

And, as the world turned white, we began to discover visitors we had not known. Mostly, they came at night.

There was the fox, whose tracks were laid one after the other in a single file straight line down the middle of the driveway, and his tracks reappeared after each successive snowfall.

There were raccoons, still circling the house, making a stop at the corn pile and going on.

There was apparently a lone coyote whose tracks could have been mistaken for a dog's.

And of course, there were all those tracks left by our two most numerous visitors: ducks and deer.

The wood ducks had moved on, but the tenacious mallards, happy with their free corn dinners, stayed and brought their friends.

The deer, too, discovered the delights of whole corn, and every evening we were able to watch them run and cavort in play and chase others in territorial disputes.

I suppose it was bound to happen, with two species competing for food. It started one evening when at least fifty mallards tumbled out of the sky and landed, some of them head over heels, in the midst of half a dozen deer.

The deer, thinking it was raining, or perhaps snowing, ducks, scattered, leaving the corn to the feathered horde. Soon, however, they recovered their courage and began to move back toward the food. Now, it was the ducks who scattered, most of them taking wing, while a few scooted away reluctantly.

The deer had no real problem with a few ducks waddling about on the ground. But those four-pound corn-fed cannonballs in the air were something else. The flock looped twice, set their wings at treetop level and dropped into the herd. Again, the deer scattered, and ducks retook their prize.

We watched as the conflict seesawed with victory in doubt. Though much smaller, the ducks worked in unison and achieved success through numbers. The deer moved along and finally decided, "Who needs this aggravation?" and left the ducks in control.

❉ ❉ ❉

I thought back to a few weeks earlier when, on one lovely afternoon, we were bouncing along a rutted and corduroyed old logging road that ran through low, swampy country. I had purchased a duck stamp along with my hunting license but had not used it.

And then, alongside the road through the cattails, I spied a mallard's green head sitting on a small pond. It was more than I could resist, so I pulled out the twenty-gauge, slipped in a shell and eased out of the Jeep. He flew just as I brought the gun up. Lucky shot!

I opened the tailgate and urged Ramah to get the splashing duck. She ran to the water's edge and stopped, eager but not willing to plunge in.

Seeing the duck twenty-five feet from shore, Patti got out and went to the dog, but Ramah was not going out there. So, Patti, dressed in blue jeans and tennis shoes, went and was soon up to her hips in mud and water.

"What are you doing?" I yelled in astonishment.

"We've got to get the duck," she replied.

"Let the dog get it," I shouted.

"She's not going to."

"Oh, jeez, you'll catch pneumonia," I said. "The duck's not worth it."

She kept going, finally up to her waist in the icy waters before she could reach the mallard and start back.

Soaked, shoes black with mud, she returned to the car with duck in hand and dog trotting behind.

"Why did you do that?" I asked. "I could have got him some other way. He'd have floated to shore."

"Floated? You mean he wouldn't sink?" She looked at me with confusion in her eyes.

"No, he wouldn't have sunk," I replied, then brightened, "but you make a heck of a bird dog," I laughed.

"Well, someone had to do it, and I was sure he'd sink." She said.

"I love you," I said, hugging her tight. "Now let's get that wet stuff off and wrap you in the blanket."

We went home with the mallard, which I cleaned and put in the freezer. It looked like I'd be giving it away with the partridges. My duck hunting days were obviously over, with fifty ducks frolicking on the lawn.

❋ ❋ ❋

Now that a thin cover of snow had revealed many animal visitors moving at night, I called Arrowhead Electric Co-op and asked about a yard light. They said they'd be out later in the day to install it on a pole near the garage.

As a boy, growing up in northwestern Minnesota, I knew that yard lights on farms and rural dwellings provided a comforting pool of light against the dark and isolation, well worth the small cost of electricity they burned.

So that night, the new light went on automatically to bathe the driveway and yard in a dull-green, mercury-vapor glow. After that, we could go outside at night without carrying a lantern or flashlight.

The second acquisition we'd agreed upon was a snowmobile. This was a bit more complicated, since I'd looked at the Polaris and Arctic Cat models sold locally without finding anything simple or affordable. We didn't want to go fast or spend $4,000. We wanted to go ice fishing and spend $2,000.

So we drove sixty-five miles southwest to the little village of Beaver Bay, where a dealer handled the Ski Doo brand, which offered a long track, small-engine model complete with metal carrying rack on the back but no other frills. It was call the Tundra model: orange, slow, relatively lightweight at three hundred pounds, and only $2,000. A couple of days after we'd picked out the perfect machine, cousin Ted and I went down to Beaver Bay in his pickup to horse it aboard and take it home. By then, the early snow had diminished, so we dragged it into the garage and parked it until more snow arrived.

To haul the machine behind the Jeep, I removed the rollers from the boat trailer, attached a four-by-eight-foot plywood panel with tie-down eyes and, voila, a tilt-bed snowmobile trailer.

And, of course, working in the garage led to a thorough pre-winter clean-up, which led in turn to the discovery that the garage was occupied, at least part-time, by Bertha Squirrel.

I first heard her while down in the garage cellar firing up the wood-chip furnace. She would come in via the chip conveyor opening that led to the storage room just above the furnace and boiler room. The sounds she made diminished, and I assumed she was going up to the second floor, an eighteen-foot by thirty-six storage area that warmed in the afternoon sun.

Sure enough, while I was cleaning, she would peek at me from her observation post on a heavy support joist overhead. Discovering the squirrel, I called to Patti, who came out and fed Bertha a few nuts while she unraveled the mystery.

Since the snow, Bertha had apparently moved inside, where Patti found numerous nuts and sunflower seeds stored for later. There were signs everywhere of Bertha's visits, but no damage. We put away most of the loose boots and clothing, but left our friendly companion with a nice pile of sunflower seeds and a few almonds. Although she spent a part of her time in the garage, she was also quick to defend "her" back deck. When either Patti or I went outside, Bertha was instantly on hand to greet us.

After the first snowfall of any consequence in early November, we went out to shovel the back deck. Zip! There was Bertha, ready to help. By then, Patti and the little squirrel had become close friends, with Bertha crawling up Patti's pant leg or sitting on her lap. So I suppose it was only natural that when Patti took over pushing the snow shovel across the deck, Bertha wanted to get involved. That's exactly what happened; when Patti stopped a moment, the squirrel leaped up onto the top of the shovel blade as if to ride along.

"Bertha, get off the shovel," Patti said gently, removing her by hand and putting her up on the bench where she would be safe. When Bertha made another attempt to jump back up on the moving snow shovel, I suggested it might be time for me to take over.

"I don't think she trusts me enough to try that while I'm pushing the shovel," I said, still laughing over our aggressive and playful little friend.

Sure enough, she kept her distance when I pushed snow.

4

❄ Traditions ❄

As deer season approached, there was snow inland, near our house, but none down below, near Lake Superior. Deer hunting had been something of a family tradition in my life and I had hunted on opening day in the same place from 1953, when I was fifteen, until 1972, the year my dad died. He and his four brothers and their sons of hunting age would gather the evening before the season for a dinner, then hunt together on opening day. It was like a family reunion that occurred no matter what else might be happening. I drove from as far away as Milwaukee to participate, and one of my cousins scheduled a military furlough so he could be there.

In the fifties, when I started hunting, there were many more deer in the area and many more hunters. Along every back road, you could find camps full of hunters who returned, year after year, to the same place, just as we did. The reason for more deer was less timber. Yes, despite the illusions of environmentalists, there are many more large trees these days than thirty or forty years ago, when the habitat favored the deer. Instead of seeing a town full of red-clad hunters, as was once the case, there are only a few, mostly locals.

Still, I was determined to hunt if only for the excuse to spend a few days in the woods. I called a couple of cousins,

Ted and Mike, and found out they, along with Mike's dad John, would be at their usual posts on opening day. Only four of us; once we had been ten or more.

The alarm woke us at 4:00 A.M., and I got out our orange-wool wardrobe while Patti made coffee. We talked a bit about the weather conditions, below freezing and calm, and then climbed into the Jeep and set off. The two bucks, Big and Little, were standing alongside the driveway when we pulled out, and I rolled down the window and shooed them away as we passed. We had already named our property "The Sanctuary," and that meant protection for all the creatures that came along.

There was a fair amount of traffic that morning, hunters moving about, and we went four miles west of Grand Marais on Highway 61. From there, we traveled uphill half a mile on foot with a flashlight. We were still smokers in those days, so we were winded and hot when we reached the stump where I had stood so many times over the years. Patti and I had reconnoitered the site a week earlier and nailed a new seat board onto the rotting old stump that had been there thirty-five years earlier when I first hunted. We had also cleared some brush that interfered with movement.

Standing quietly in the woods while the world awakens is to know what the enjoyment of hunting is all about. It truly did not matter whether a large buck came along or not; in fact when he did a day later, I enjoyed the excitement but did not shoot.

It is probably a proven truth that in Minnesota cold, the hotter one gets walking through the woods, the colder that person will get when standing perfectly still. So, as each species awakens and adds voice to the woods, I will be starting to shake. By the time daylight broke and the crows, ravens, jays, and squirrels start advertising my presence to everyone and everything within earshot, I was hopping from foot to foot and might just as well be wandering around breaking brush underfoot.

For Patti, the most amazing thing was that in the cold silence, the wings of ravens and crows passing overhead actually sounded loud as they sliced the air. Even a chickadee wing beats could easily be heard as it flew from limb to limb.

From where we stood several hundred feet above Lake Superior, the huge lake spread away into infinity and we could actually see the curve in the earth. The sun, just a shade lighter than our red-orange hunting clothes, made a spectacular panorama as it seemed to rise out of the inland sea.

As we spent time watching and listening in the woods, we gained acuity. The sound of tall grass waving, for example, differs from the sound of the same grass being pushed aside by a walking deer. Animal and human faces begin to look out of place against the shapes of nature.

Standing silently, we heard a faint, birdlike peep-peep-peep. Turning heads slowly, we scanned along the ground and spotted a partridge, his neck craned alertly. He stepped forward, claws extended, exaggerated stealth in each movement. Dry leaves rustled. Another, no, two more grouse—a covey of three. This was near the peak of their ten-year cycle, so the birds were abundant.

I thought back over the years and wondered how many grouse I had seen while sitting right in that very place. Fifty? A hundred? Probably more. They came and went through the days, as did squirrels, foxes, rabbits and even moose.

It was 1953 when I first followed my dad to the stand.

"Stand right here," he said, "and keep your eyes open. Leave the safety on until you're ready to shoot."

At that moment, I was shaking from the excitement and tension. This was an occasion I'd awaited for years, and suddenly my mind was blank. "Which way should I look?" I whispered.

"Mostly down below, but keep checking behind you too. Move real slow, like I showed you" he added. "I'll be back

about nine," and he was gone into the darkness, moving
silently up the trail without a light.

Alone in the dark in the woods, I was afraid. What if a
moose came thundering down the trail? Suppose a bear
crept up on me. Even a big buck deer with sharp antlers
could decide to attack. And wolves, well, you never know
how many shots I could get off as the pack attacked. I started at every sound and nearly leaped from my skin when at
earliest light, a shot echoed across the ridge. My first job
that morning was to find a climbable tree, just in case my
worst fears materialized, which, of course, they never did.

I spent nine cold mornings there that first year and
learned to distinguish many of the sights and sounds of
deer season, but the only sign of deer I saw were the tracks
I would find each morning by flashlight along the trail I
used to hike from the highway to the road.

The second year, at age sixteen, I found many signs of deer
near the cabin on the day before the season and begged my
dad to let me hunt there instead of on the ridge. He looked
hard at me, then agreed without comment. At 8:30 A.M., the
horn of a car started blaring through the woods. It was coming from the direction of the cabin, so I hurried back, to find
a pickup in the yard. It was Uncle Wes. "C'mon sport," he
hollered as I came into view. "You've got some work to do."

As we drove west on Highway 61, he told me how my dad
had shot five deer right at daylight. My mouth fell open.

"Where was he?" I asked.

"In your stand," he said, glancing at me over his glasses
with a grin.

With five deer already in camp, we were halfway to filling
out our permits, a rare event. I spent the next three hours
dragging deer down the hill, and of course I spent every possible moment during the rest of the season in that very
stand, again without seeing a deer.

As the seasons passed, one year warm and sunny, the next
white with blowing snow, I learned about the woods and the

habits of not only deer and other creatures but also of my fellow hunters who inhabited the woods for two weeks in November. For most, the deer they took home each season was a source of food for the winter. But as Patti and I sat looking into the mixed tangle of birch, poplar, and brush around us, we were content to leave each afternoon empty-handed. We much preferred watching the deer, and these "hunting" trips were understood to be for the purpose of observation only. There were no chances to shoot. One day, making a small loop around the area where we hunted, I stopped in a glade darkened by large cedars and half a dozen old white pines. The cathedral-like silence was broken by the crunch of a twig as a large buck stepped into the open. He passed directly in front of me, following a scent trail, and I watched silently as he picked his way through the forest litter and was gone. At that moment, the experience of enjoying this beautiful animal's passage easily surpassed the idea of his rack mounted on a wall or of his meat in our freezer.

❆ ❆ ❆

Whether deer hunting or simply driving the back roads, we tried to spend time each day exploring our new home. One day, we stopped for lunch at a Poplar Lake resort that featured furniture made of diamond willow, a tree found in swampy areas and distinctive for its dark "diamonds" set against light wood.

Patti immediately wanted to get some in its natural state to make us a couple of walking sticks. So we asked our wood expert, Phil Hedstrom, when he came to visit and check over the furnace one day.

"Oh sure, you bet. Hop in the truck, and we'll go get some right now," he answered enthusiastically.

So we set off and in less than a mile came to a marshy area which he described as "a good spot."

"Okay," he said pointing. "Right through there is a clump. Take the Swede saw in back and go cut one."

Patti set out eagerly with saw in hand, and when she got back in the thicket about thirty yards, she pointed questioningly at a sapling.

"No. No." Phil responded, pointing more to the left.

Patti moved and pointed again. Phil shrugged. His eyes weren't all that great anymore. Patti started sawing and soon was proudly squishing through the snow-covered mush with a six-foot stick in hand.

"Oh, oh," Phil muttered as she approached.

"Well?" She asked, smiling proudly and holding the stick up for inspection.

"It's a dandy," he smiled. "In fact, it may be the best-looking alder stick I've ever seen."

"You mean it's not . . . ?"

"Nope, afraid you picked an alder instead of willow. But go back and try again. That's willow in there, sure as shootin'."

She decided against another trip through the marsh that day but cheered up when Phil assured her diamond willow grew right along some of the back roads, "so close you could reach out and touch the stuff."

True to his words, he appeared the next morning with a couple of lengths of the real stuff in his pickup. When stripped of bark and varnished to show the contrast between light wood and almost black "diamonds," the willow did indeed make durable, striking walking sticks.

❋ ❋ ❋

Deer hunting starts each year with a bang—workers taking days off, coffee shop discussions of favored hunting locations, church dinners, big deer contests, and such—and ends quietly. That's because as hunters either bag their deer or get their fill of the cold and woods, they just stop hunting. By the last few days of the season, the fact that the hunt is still underway is easily missed.

And then of course, by the end of deer hunting, Thanksgiving is at the threshold, with its family dinners and holiday hoopla. This year, for the first time in many years, Patti and I were drawn into the wonderful warmth of a big, extended family for the holidays. We joined several cousins and their spouses and children for Thanksgiving dinner in town.

"So how are you doing up there in the woods?" One asked.

"No problems so far," I replied confidently.

"Well, it's been warm so far. It'll start getting cold with a lot more snow soon," he said.

"So, when are you going to Florida?" Asked a female cousin whose parents were already wintering there.

"We're not, unless you count a couple of weeks later in the winter," I assured her. "We're having a great time at our house in the woods."

At that statement, several skeptical glances turned my way. Minnesotans may have this perverse pride at being able to get through the winter, but they also think a trip to Florida, or even Arizona during that time, is the closest they'll ever get to paradise. And right then, they were trying to figure out what had possessed us to move back there with the idea of spending the winter, all six or seven months of it.

"We love it here," Patti said. "All our new animal and bird friends. There's never a dull moment with Bertha Squirrel, Chester the Chipmunk, or Percy Partridge."

Suddenly, their interest was hooked, or maybe they politely thought we were nuts. Patti forged ahead telling of our adventures with some of the creatures who lived near our house.

That day we realized that although we lived in the midst of a near wilderness, many lifelong residents simply took it for granted or had lost interest.

"I haven't seen a moose in years," one lady said. "But then I haven't been out in the woods for years either. I spend my free time at the mall in Duluth."

Everyone laughed and conversation spun off in a new direction. That night, Patti and I rehashed the day's events, which had been wonderful. But we agreed to mutual surprise that many had developed a "done that, been there," attitude toward the woods.

"They'd rather watch TV or shop than go out in the woods," I said. "For them, the woods has always been here. It's just part of the scenery. They really don't see it anymore."

"We go looking for moose and see several every month," I added. "If you don't go looking you won't see any. The same with bears and the other animals. Except for the deer, you won't find many of them standing out on the highway."

"One thing is certain. Everyone agrees you've got a special gift with animals, and that fascinates them."

Patti rolled her eyes to downplay the compliment. "Hey, I just like animals."

"Right," I laughed. "That's why we've got four cats."

❋ ❋ ❋

The next morning, we awoke to a couple more inches of new snow. It was not unexpected. We had several inches on the ground, and the winter was just underway. I went out and swept the back deck while Patti put out sunflower seeds along the railings and in the box for the birds. The food soon attracted two squirrels, which sat at opposite ends of the railing like bookends, plus a dozen or more evening grosbeaks, which resembled small green parrots. Although these were beautiful birds with an appropriate name, their behavior was raucous and rude. Their cousins, the red-trimmed pine grosbeaks, were much more civil and considerate. At present, however, we had a covey of the green variety and only a few of the more placid and quiet reds.

The grosbeaks were now joined by other early winter regulars: chickadees, nuthatches, juncos, and blue jays. An interesting fact—although we occasionally saw some gray or Canadian jays, legendary among loggers and other woodsman for their friendly and easy-to-tame personalities, they never joined the other birds in our feeders.

The phone was ringing when we went inside. It was my uncle Sid.

"We're going out to get Princess Pine," he said. "Got to pick 'em before we get any more snow. You guys want to come along?"

My mind went blank. "Princess Pine. What's that?" I asked.

"Yah, you know the stuff to make wreaths at the church."

"Oh, sure, okay, just a minute," I cupped my hand over the receiver to ask Patti a question to which I already knew the answer. "You want to go with Sid and Betty to get some of the pine they make wreaths out of?"

Her eyes lit up. "Oh, yes, yes. I need to make three or four if Betty will show me how."

Adult evening grosbeak feeding full-grown baby. They do that all winter.

So we met Sid and Betty and went up the Bally Creek Road in search of Princess Pine, which grows like a miniature pine about six or eight inches tall and is difficult to spot. It's like picking blueberries; you either get down close on your hands and knees or you don't see them.

We hunted two or three hours and got enough to fill a couple of big black plastic bags. According to Betty, it was enough to make half a dozen Christmas wreaths. Compared to wreaths made of regular pine or spruce, these are special, the best. They stay green and they don't shed.

After collecting the little pines, we got a basic lesson in wreath construction and went home to start work in the garage. By mid-afternoon, Patti had created three wreaths that I thought spectacular, complete with large, red, satin bows. Our constant companion in this enterprise was Bertha squirrel, who sat and watched and got an occasional nut for her interest.

While we worked in the garage, a light snowfall started. It was very fine in texture, and I was reminded of the old saying, "snow like meal, snow a great deal." With Lake Superior nearby, unexpected heavy snow sometimes came in on an east wind. I had talked to a local trucker who told me that he set out from Grand Marais one day a couple of winters earlier. By the time he stopped fifty-five miles away at Silver Bay and took shelter, three feet of snow had fallen. Silver Bay ended up with forty-six inches of snow, and Grand Marais had none.

Once past Thanksgiving in northern Minnesota, winter comes on fast. It's no longer a question of whether it will be rain or snow; it will be snow. The question is how much. This snow thickened and intensified and became our first real snow of the year. Patti and I took Ramah for a walk with flashlights down the driveway. The dog romped and ate snow while we held gloved hands and felt the wet flakes on our faces. Ahead lay snow unmarked by any prints, like blank white paper. By dawn, tracks in the snow would reveal the comings and goings of nocturnal animals that had passed our way in the night.

We awakened to a sparkling fairyland of snow and our first below-zero temperatures. It was also a morning to load chips from the truck onto the conveyor where they would travel into the chip storage room. We went out with our shovels to the chip truck and were immediately faced with a new problem. Until now, we had used a small shovel to dislodge the chips so they fell onto the floor of the truck where we could push them with a wide shovel into the maw of the conveyor. It went fast. Now, however, all the moisture from earlier rains and the previous night's snow and cold had caused the chips to freeze into a solid mass. The small shovel wouldn't loosen even a single chip of wood. I stood there staring at a glacier of chips seven feet high and about eight feet wide and knew the feeling of despair.

"How do we do this?" Patti asked.

I thought a minute and said, "with a pick, just like a couple of miners." I climbed down, waded back through the snow to the garage and returned with a rusty pick. After two or three blows into the frozen mass, I knew this was going to be hard work, miserable work.

We took turns with pick and shovel, for an hour working up a sweat in spite of the cold. Then we stood back and admired our "mine," which was two feet deep, four feet wide and almost six feet high. It was another twenty feet to the front of the truck. By mid-winter, we would hollow out the contents and laughingly call our hard work, "The Elbow Creek Mine," but the work never got any easier. By then, the sun had lost its punch and could offer little melting power, and the thermometer was always freezing or below. It was dig or pay astronomical electric bills to heat the water that warmed the house. We dug, smug in our calculation that we were saving about fifteen dollars for every hour we spent outside.

Hairy woodpecker at suet ball.

5

❄ Dazed Bird, Thin Ice, Big Tree ❄

At the advice of neighbors, we hung suet balls, really no more than fat from the butcher at Johnson's Store tied in a string bag, from the branches of the cherry tree directly in front of the dining room windows. Many of the winter birds, jays and chickadees especially, enjoyed the suet in their winter diet. But the ones who spent the most time pecking at these treats were the woodpeckers of all sizes, from small downy to mid-sized hairy to the large, prehistoric-looking pileated woodpeckers. We had been told the pileated woodpeckers were very shy and unlikely to visit our suet. Another myth: these angular, red-cockaded birds became very nearly daily visitors. They sometimes finished off their dinner with a few loud taps on the house, which sounded like a carpenter driving nails in the wood siding.

One day just past Thanksgiving, we were sprawled in the family room reading and heard a loud "thunk." It was followed almost immediately, by a second, even louder "thunk." We had heard this sound before, the crash of a bird against the window.

We ran out into the snow, and the story unfolded. There in the front yard were two birds, a hairy woodpecker and a large hawk. The hawk was staggering about as if he'd been dealt a near-knockout blow. The woodpecker lay silent in the snow. It

Pileated woodpecker—we had several.

was obvious that the hawk, who should have migrated by now, had pursued the woodpecker into the upstairs window. Sometimes birds became confused by reflections in the glass and guessed that it showed a opening into the forest. To reduce collisions, we hung branches from the top of the outside frame. We had never before seen a woodpecker have this problem, but these had apparently been desperate circumstances.

After one look at the big hawk, who was by now scooting away through the snow using his wings as paddles, Patti went for the woodpecker. It was a female, about the size of a large blue jay.

"I don't think she's going to make it," Patti said, cradling the bird in her hands while gently breathing warm air on it.

The hawk recovered quickly and flew to a nearby branch for further rest. The woodpecker began to move a bit but without any seeming consciousness. And then after about five minutes of warming and quiet talk, the bird began to wake up. Eyes that had been glazed were now sharp and alert.

Suddenly, Patti realized her face was only inches away from a woodpecker with a sharp, two-inch-long beak. But the bird made no attempt to fly, just sat quietly as it recovered its awareness. When she felt the time was right, Patti opened her hands and let the woodpecker stand alone.

"Go with God," she said, and the hairy fluttered up to a small branch in the cherry tree above. It sat there for quite a few minutes before flying off. When we looked around for the hawk, it, too, had disappeared.

The next morning, when Patti put out seeds on the stump in front, a female hairy woodpecker flew about her, then landed overhead in the cherry tree, where it sat peeping.

She looked at the bird and asked it, "Are you the little girl who got hurt yesterday?" Apparently it was, and she began to appear almost every time Patti was out in front putting out food or shoveling the walk.

Woodpeckers do not migrate and were among our year-round bird neighbors, along with blue jays, chickadees, grosbeaks, owls, and nuthatches. At first we were amazed to see the hawk, since most of them migrate in late September. However, we learned from one of the local birders that a new group of predators, owls and hawks, were starting to come down from the far north. It was common for this to happen every few years, and, by January, we would be in the middle of a full-scale invasion.

❊ ❊ ❊

After the snowfall, we took the snowmobile out for a couple of rides on the back roads and on trails through the nearby woods. It was time for our first ice-fishing expedition. We

Ice-fishing scene.

chose Mit Lake, first lake on the Ball Club Road, where we'd caught several nice walleyes during the summer.

We arrived at the Ball Club Road, which led to a remote section of woods and lakes, and discovered it had not been plowed. We parked and set out on our trusty orange Tundra, which we had named Orange Julius. The last mile to the lake was over a rock logging road, which the snow made more easily navigable, and we were soon at the shore of Mit Lake.

Nobody had been there since earlier in the fall, before the snow. There is always an edge of tension that accompanies me when I know I am truly alone in the woods. There probably wasn't a person for several miles, and I recognized that fact as we set out across the ice.

We reached the open part of the lake, and I suggested we try an island that had been productive in the summer. The route lay across a wind-swept area of ice that looked like clear glass.

"Wait, don't go." Patti burst out. "Are you sure about the ice? It doesn't look thick enough."

Just then, as if to put a point on her concern, the ice cracked loudly.

"Oh, oh," she warned. "I'm not going out there."

"There's nothing to fear," I said. "That ice is several inches thick. It just looks thin. That crack is a sign the lake is 'making ice,' as they say. That the ice is getting thicker."

"Is it thick enough to hold us?" She asked, still fearful.

"Six inches will hold a truck," I said reassuringly. "A foot will hold a railroad car."

I began to cut through the ice with the hand auger and soon discovered about six inches of ice. Plenty for snowmobile travel but less than I expected, considering the cold.

We went across the quarter mile of clear ice fast and parked along the wooded shore. I drilled two holes in exactly the same places we had anchored the canoe the previous summer and then set the lines baited with minnows down near the rocky bottom.

Then we waited and waited. I made a small wood fire, and we cooked hot dogs on sticks. In the cold air, they were delicious.

We waited and waited some more. A north wind sprang up, blowing snow-trails across the clear black ice. It got colder. We put up our parka hoods and sat with our backs to the wind. The ice cracked ominously. The call of a wolf, lonely on the wind, blew toward us from the north. A second wolf joined in.

"Well, what do you think?" I asked. "Doesn't look like we'll do any good. Feels like it could snow. Want to hang it up?"

"Sure, I'm ready if you are. Maybe we just need to try some other places. Maybe the fish live in different parts of the lake in the winter."

Hearing the wolves and adding that chill to the one I already felt was enough to set me in action. I quickly had the hand lines pulled up. Patti brought the pack sack, we secured it with bungee cords. I switched on the machine and grabbed the starter rope.

"Sure hope it starts," I teased.

"Bite your tongue," she answered.

The rasping engine caught on the second pull, as always, and we were off through the blowing snow.

❋ ❋ ❋

By the time we arrived home, snow again fell silently in large, cottony flakes. A few deer stood near the remnants of the corn pile, wearing white blankets of snow on their backs. They appeared to be does and fawns. After hunting season, we had seen Big Buck on at least two occasions, but of Little Buck, there was no sign.

We worried that, through our friendliness, we had somehow caused Little Buck to lose his fear and become an easier target for a hunter. Perhaps, instead of bolting, the young deer had stood watching as he often did with us. Patti and I talked about this question but had not yet found an answer. Other than the missing Little Buck, our small herd seemed to be in fine health.

With the coming of cold weather and Patti's natural bent to cook, our table saw a rapid expansion of foods and recipes. Italian chicken and pasta dishes, old Swedish favorites, new ideas, all found their way to our table. The only problem that this surge of culinary activity caused was a need for more storage space. I spent a couple of evenings building shelves in the basement out of one-by-twelves we found in the garage. With another thirty-five feet of shelving, Patti assured me she could make due for a while.

❄ ❄ ❄

Living in the land of spruce, pine, and balsam, we had been scouting the area for likely sources for our first real Christmas tree. Although they sold trees for about ten or fifteen dollars in town, we were determined to get our own.

But it's one thing to go to a tree lot and select from pines that have been trimmed and shaped each year, entirely another to find a shapely specimen in the wild. We snowmobiled up one likely logging trail and down another, but nothing seemed just right. A lot of the nice-looking trees turned out, on close inspection, to have double trunks, sort of like two trees in one.

Finally, about fifteen miles up the Gunflint Trail, we discovered an area full of spruce trees, our favorite short-needle variety of conifer. The area was also full of moose, judging from the huge tracks dug deep into the snow. As we traveled, looking for a tree, we realized the snow was at least thirty inches deep there, about three times the depth at home.

Off on a hillside about a hundred yards distant, we spotted what appeared to be the perfect tree. We drove over for a closer look, then waded and struggled through the deep snow to stand beside it.

"Terrific," I enthused. It looked about eight feet tall, which would be perfect in our A-frame living room. So, out came the saw, and I pushed aside the snow to get down close to the ground on the trunk.

We towed the tree easily behind the snowmobile back to the road and tied it with bungee cords to the roof rack of the Jeep. It already seemed larger than it had when we looked at it out in the snow. No problem, I thought. We can handle that. It's a big open room. With the tree safely home in the garage, I got out our Christmas tree stand. Hmmm, I mused. The stand, with its four-inch trunk capacity, looked like a miniature against our tree's six-inch-diameter trunk. And when we stood it upright, the tree was eleven feet tall.

"Maybe we could cut it down a bit," Patti suggested.

There didn't seem to be much choice, so I agreed. "And we'll have to see if they make bigger stands," I added.

For the next couple of days, the tree waited in the garage as I searched around town for an adequate tree holder. Finally, an unlikely source, the lumber yard, came up with one that looked like it would accommodate five and one-half inches. After cutting off more than two feet at the bottom, the trunk fit snugly, and we raised the still-large spruce to its full height of nearly nine feet in the garage and began to feed it sugar water.

At that time, I was reminded that cousin Ted had suggested marking the right tree before the snow came. Otherwise, he explained, the tree will be down in the snow and you'll get home with a much bigger tree than you expected.

After all this, those twelve-dollar trees down at the Holiday station were starting to look much more attractive.

❄ ❄ ❄

By the end of November, some of the more accessible lakes—Devil's Track and Poplar, to name two—were frozen over and had become snowmobile raceways, while others were dotted with ice fishermen. Only a couple of the largest lakes, Gunflint and Greenwood, remained free of ice.

At home, Elbow Creek slowly narrowed as ice built out from both banks. One morning, when I stepped out on the back deck to help Patti with a new fifty-pound bag of sunflower seeds, I was aware of a conspicuous silence. It took a moment to understand that the creek had sealed over with ice and snow. All our time in this house had been accompanied by the sound of running water, sometimes roaring, other times a lovely gurgle. The quiet was strikingly different.

"Do you hear it?" I asked.

Patti listened, "What?"

"The silence," I said, pointing down below at the frozen surface of the creek.

"That's what it is," she smiled. "I knew there was something strange."

We stood listening to the cold silence, then a blue jay called and a squirrel chattered.

"Nothing quiet about Bertha," Patti laughed, watching our little red friend scamper across the snow and climb up onto the deck. Bertha went directly to Patti, who gave her a nut, as expected.

We went inside, and I was in the den writing bills when Patti called excitedly. "Jack, come quick, There's a strange animal in the cherry tree."

"What kind of animal?" I responded.

"I don't know," she whispered loudly, "but it looks sort of like a monkey."

I gave her one of those rolled-eye looks, as if to say, "monkey indeed," wondering if winter was getting to her, then followed her dutifully to peek around the corner.

At first glance, watching the animal stretch between tree branch and suet ball, it did look like some kind of monkey, event though I knew it to be a pine marten, a small but fierce member of the weasel family.

I identified the marten for Patti and explained that it could run like a squirrel through the trees, that in fact it often chased and caught squirrels. I went on to say we'd have to move the suet to a new, more inaccessible location since it had been discovered by the marten.

I looked at Patti to see her eyes tearing. She daubed them and shook her head. "What will become of Bertha?" She asked in a shaken voice.

"Maybe I should scare the pine marten so he doesn't feel like he has discovered a new home." I said. "Then I'll move the suet."

A pine marten in action is one fearless little beast. I got outside and hollered, only to have it growl back at me. Whoa, I thought and reached down to make a snowball.

Two near misses set the marten into action and it went leaping through the trees from branch to branch like Tarzan. An amazing but dangerous little animal.

We hung the suet on strings under the eaves, where we figured even a marten would have trouble reaching it. The birds seemed happy with the new location, which was important, so I was satisfied.

That night, our beautiful but deadly visitor returned. I awoke to hear something scratching at the A-frame roof and eaves and got up to look out at the bright night caused by the reflection of moonlight on the snow.

The marten hung from the eave, trying to stretch under the overhanging roof far enough to reach the suet's string, which he would then pull up to get at the suet. Like a contortionist, he was somehow holding onto the roof while attempting all this.

Quietly, I got a flashlight and went downstairs, then outside to scare him again. This time, he fled without resistance or reward. I somehow felt, accurately as it turned out, that we would see more of this bold fellow during the winter.

6

❄ Cold Enough ❄

With the advent of really cold weather, the deer mice moved inside, where they were confronted by four determined cats. At night, we would hear the mice moving in the walls, and all four cats waited silently for them to appear.

Three of our cats, Einstein, Booter, and Caesar, had little trouble catching them, but they were so well fed that they had no interest in eating them. Instead they would bring the captives and deposit them, alive and generally in good health, right next to the bed. There the frightened little mouse would make a dash for freedom, setting off yet another chase.

Patti and I were awakened by this chaos several times in just a few nights. We would get up, shoo the cats, capture the confused mouse in a shoebox and take him to the basement where he was free to roam without cat interference.

Our fourth cat, Sammy, had only three legs and at first seemed unable to catch a mouse. Then one night, we were awakened by Sammy sitting on the bed, meowing loudly. When we sat up, he lifted his one front paw and out ran a mouse, straight for Patti. Seeing Sammy's gift running towards her, Patti yelled and tossed the covers. The mouse flew, the cat ran for it, and before the covers landed, we both were out of bed with lights on.

The four cats. Left to right: Einstein, Sammy, Caesar, and Boots.

Fortunately, we discovered the mouse, still alive, among the tangled sheets and blankets and took him downstairs for a second chance.

A deer mouse resembles a cartoon character with big ears and soft dark eyes. Often, the reaction to seeing one isn't "rodent" but "cute little animal." I find myself motivated to protect them from the cats.

At night, we set the thermostat in the house at sixty degrees. When the wood-chip burner went out at about 10:00 P.M., we turned on the electrical elements to heat the five-hundred gallon tank of water as needed.

The electricity for the heating system was designated "interruptible" and could be turned off by the power company when needed elsewhere, as during a very cold spell. By agreeing to this, we got the power for 3.5 cents per watt instead of the regular eight-cent rate. Up to that point, if they had turned it off at night, we hadn't even noticed.

This had become a nightly routine that worked to perfection, and we already took it for granted. That was mistake number one. Along came a cold night, about twenty below zero, with a strong north wind. We could hear trees, frozen and stiff, cracking as they swayed.

With the wood-chip burner, when we went to bed, we were comfortable inside our snug house and laughingly said it was not a fit night out for man or beast. Then we slid beneath the quilts without another thought.

It was still dark when Patti roused me, saying, "Jack, get up. There's something wrong with the heat."

We went downstairs, saw with horror that the thermometer read forty-eight degrees in the house and agreed there was a problem. It was a simple one—no electricity to heat the water. Apparently, it had been off all night.

I lit a big, crackling fire in the fireplace, then went out through the garage and descended into the basement to start up the chip burner. Within about four hours, the house was back up to its normal daytime temperature, but I still felt cold. A hot shower warmed me throughout and, thereafter, when we got really chilled, inside and out, we solved the problem in this way.

In my younger years I don't recall ever having a problem dealing with the extreme cold. Fortunately, our hot shower was especially successful in solving this, since it was fitted with fiberglass walls and ceiling to trap the heat inside. I could literally feel myself thaw.

After experiencing this interruption of power for the first time, we were more watchful of our heating system. If the weather was especially cold and the interruptible electricity was off, we ran the chip burner until nearly midnight and got up early to get it started. We found that to be a simple solution that kept early morning temperatures in the mid-fifties in all but the most brutal conditions.

❋ ❋ ❋

That morning, after warming up, we went out to take the dog for a walk. At minus fifteen or twenty, we started to take precautions we wouldn't bother taking at fifteen or twenty above because there's a big difference.

At twenty below, we couldn't just throw on a jacket and slip Sorels over bare feet to go out for a few minutes. That feeling that comes when one takes a big bite of ice cream is what it feels like to gulp in that super-cold air. The bite of the frozen air gave me a coughing spell if I got too much at once. With some people, it's headaches, with others, pain, and when a bit of wind is added, the cold knifes right through any unprotected places.

But Ramah needed to go out, so we both accompanied her. Patti put on long johns and insulated snow pants, two pair of socks and Sorel arctic boots, a sweater, super heavy parka, choppers (leather mitts with thick wool liners) a scarf and a musher's cap with ear flaps. My fashion statement was about the same, except I pulled on a one-piece insulated snowmobile suit and a Russian-style fur hat.

Outside, the air was silent, and our breath hung in clouds around us. We started down the packed snow of the driveway, and every step squeaked and creaked. The sounds echoed through the trees. Certainly no stealth was possible even if we had tried.

We covered a hundred yards, moving clumsily in our heavy clothing, then Patti noted that Ramah was holding up a paw. She was game, but she was also a Florida lab, and this was cold. It was time for us to turn and head back.

The fire in the fireplace was still burning, and the smoke wreathed the chimney top and rose lazily into the sky, where it seemed to hang. In Grand Marais, where many people still burned wood, such a morning would cause the smoke to cast a pall over the entire town. At the school, the smoke column from the tall chimney rose half a mile or more.

At minus twenty, a car should be in a garage or plugged in to keep the oil or the engine block warm. Otherwise, one was likely to go out, wrestle the frozen door open, get in and sit on the rock hard seat, turn the key and listen to that depressing sound: Rrrrr, rrrr, rrrr, silence. Rrrrr, rrrr, silence. Click, silence. Then all one can do is just sit there as one's breath makes frost on the inside of the windshield and try to remember where the jumper cables were left last. No, there's nothing forgiving about twenty below, but in northern Minnesota, life goes on. At forty below, it's a different story, as we would discover.

⁂ ⁂ ⁂

We knew there was a pair of ravens around because we'd see them and hear their distinctive calls from time to time. One day while Patti was outside, she saw a raven sitting high in a tree above her, seemingly talking to her in a gutteral voice.

She came down the driveway and clunked into the house. "What do ravens eat?" she asked.

The question caught me off guard. "Huh," I exclaimed. "I think they're carnivores, at least partly, so they probably eat some meat."

"Pot roast, do you suppose?" She asked, with her head in the refrigerator.

"I don't know. Try it and see."

So out she went, striding down the driveway with pieces of pot roast in hand. When she got under the tall poplar where the raven waited, she sprinkled the meat on the waist-deep snow pile left by the plow.

As she backed away, I stepped into the doorway to see what would happen.

"Come and get it," she called. The bird looked down and studied the proposition. It was obviously interested.

She looked back at me and asked, "What would you call a raven?"

The answer was obvious, "Poe," I said.

"Good idea," she answered, turning back to where the bird peered down at the morsels.

"Okay, Poe, come on down and eat. Poe, do you hear me? Dinnertime." She talked like this to the bird for half a minute, then the raven soared down to the lowest branch, where he took up a new station.

"Come on now, Poe. I know you're hungry," she said, continuing to try to make some kind of contact.

Suddenly, the bird was down on the snow, pecking at the pieces she had left. After a few bites, he uttered a guttural squawk.

"I think he wants more," she said, pushing past me into the house. Then she returned and went outside with a bowlful of supplies.

I'll never know how she does this, but she can get inside an animal's or bird's head in a flash, and the next thing I knew, they somehow understood each other. It was amazing.

So it was with Poe. When Patti approached, he flew up only to the lowest branch, then dropped down to check out the offering as she returned. All the while, she talked to him and, amazingly, he talked back in guttural tones.

I stood shaking my head as she came back toward the house.

"Is something wrong?" She asked. "He's very hungry, you know. Maybe he'll bring his mate along for a snack next time. That's what I'm hoping."

Later that day, it warmed up, and we made a trip to town for supplies. When we returned, a raven flew down through the trees ahead of us and seemed to lead us along the road. He flew at eye level above the snowy road, then swooped up into his favorite tree.

"Poe, do you suppose?" I asked, surprised at the encounter.

"I'm sure it is," she answered matter-of-factly. "I'll take him out a few treats. I have a hunch he'll like chicken."

Poe gobbled up part of a chicken wing, then flew off with a leg. "I'll bet he's taking it to his mate," Patti said, turning for the house.

"How is it you know all this about ravens?" I asked.

She glanced at me and shrugged, then continued toward the garage to open the back door of the Jeep, where the grocery sacks were stacked.

I was still pondering about the ravens when I finished carrying groceries, so I looked down the driveway to see if Poe had come back. Sure enough, he had returned. At least I suspected that it was the same bird. With him was a second raven.

"Snooks," I called. "There are two ravens where you put the chicken. Come and take a look."

She hurried into the dining room, where she studied the two ravens with the big seven-by-fifty Fujinon binoculars.

"That must be his mate," she said. "They mate soon, during winter, and she'll be on the nest. Then in about February, they have their babies and spend the spring raising them. They stay together like geese do."

I looked at her with raised eyebrows.

She laughed and turned back to the kitchen. "It's in the bird book, if you'd bother looking."

❋ ❋ ❋

Having been built by a member of the family that owned the nearby lumber mill, our house in the woods was nearly one-hundred-percent wood, with tongue and groove black ash paneling in some areas and knotty pine in the rest. Rough-sawn, open beams crossed overhead with more knotty pine for the ceilings. It was warm and cozy-looking, the perfect home to decorate for Christmas.

And decorate we did, or I should say, Patti did, with my assistance. It was snowing steadily, and our snowbanks were now more than waist high along the driveway when I carried in the tree and set it up in the living room. After decorating for many years in the snowless warmth of Florida, this was the real thing. We played Christmas music and sang and laughed like a couple of small children. Patti had even thought to get big Christmas stockings to hang from the mantle above our stone fireplace.

When we finished inside, we still had more lights, so we set about outlining the tall A-frame with our long strings of multi-colored bulbs. Since the peaks were about thirty feet, I had no ladder tall enough and had to shinny out on the ridges and drive nails over which to suspend the strings. Once in place, they stayed year round and could be lighted in any season.

"Now that we've assembled this wonderful display of lights," I said. "Who's gonna see it?"

"Just us, I guess," Patti replied. "Unless we invite plenty of guests."

We're buried and it's not even Christmas.

So that's what we did, and our decorations were seen by thirty or more people, mostly relatives who came on Christmas Eve and Christmas Day. The lights, sparkling at night against the moonlit snow or sometimes the moving light show of the Aurora Borealis, was well worth the effort of raising and attaching them along the eaves. Several nights, we found ourselves walking with the dog a hundred yards to the curve in the driveway just to gaze on the scene from a distance.

View of the garden area and woodshed.
The peak of the shed roof is about twelve feet high.

$$\boxed{7}$$

❄ Too Much Snow ❄

With fresh snow falling from virtually every cloud that floated over, the Duluth meteorologist was moved to suggest that some kind of record snowfall for the month would be inevitable if the trend persisted. All we knew for certain was that the trail to the wood chip truck was now bordered by waist-deep snow. The lake effect, in which Lake Superior entices snow to fall when the east wind blows, was working perfectly.

All this fresh snow, which made every step feel like walking in quicksand, brought about two blunders in rapid succession.

As the flakes sparkled down in the illumination of the yard light and the Christmas lights, I began to plan the first tour by snowmobile of our winter wonderland. The first tour would be a modest forty-mile effort, involving a few miles of back country roads, a short stretch of the North Shore Trail, and then a trip north on the Gunflint Trail system to Poplar Lake, where we would stop for lunch before returning.

The next morning broke sunny and windless with above zero temperatures, a near-perfect day for winter travel. I cranked Orange Julius up and then, caught up by careless enthusiasm, did something stupid.

Why not warm up for the safari with a brief spin through our woods? I had seen enough TV commercials to believe I could glide through the white powder just like on TV. Whatever the secret of snowmobiling over deep powder, I did not have the key to unlock it. I went down the road, up over the snowbank created by the plow and into the deep powder. At that point, instead of floating in graceful S turns around the trees, Orange Julius sank like a submarine.

The only thing worse than wallowing through deep snow on a three-hundred-pound snowmobile is doing it in a four- or even five-hundred-pound model. Without something solid to bite against, the track has no traction. I couldn't move. So I lifted the back end and repositioned it. It sank again. I placed branches and small trees under the track. Maybe I moved forward a couple of feet.

As for moving a partially submerged snowmobile, a grown man can lift and reposition the track and rear end but not the front. I might as well have been lifting a pickup truck. About the only guy in Minnesota who might handle the job is the governor, and I'm sure he's smarter than that.

Anyone with a lick of sense would have turned the machine around immediately and gotten it back on solid snow. Ever the optimist, I thought if I could just get it going a bit, it would take off and start gliding, as in the commercials. Wrong again. By the time Patti noticed I was gone, I was mired down in a state of exhaustion fifty feet from the driveway, still pointing toward the hinterland.

Patti waded along the snow trail we'd carved and took a look at me. "You look gray," she said, which was probably one-hundred percent accurate, since I felt some kind of heart failure was probably imminent.

"This is impossible," I gasped. "I'll never get out."

"Sure we will," Patti encouraged. "I'll go get the Jeep, and we'll tie a line from Orange Julius to it, then drive along and pull you out."

I knew as soon as she said it that the plan would work and that in my current mental and physical state, I wouldn't have thought of it for several days.

With a hundred feet of three-quarter-inch nylon tied between the trailer hitch on the Jeep and the front rail of the snowmobile, it was easy to steer the machine back onto the road. We decided to hold back on the grand tour until a few days later, and I vowed to avoid stupid moves in the deep snow.

❅ ❅ ❅

I kept my promise until the next day. It had snowed several more inches of sparkling fluff when we got back from our trip to town for groceries. We got out of the Jeep and lifted the rear trunk lid before spotting what had to be the rump of a big moose through a screen of alders north of the yard.

"Shh," I admonished. "Go in and get the camera so we can get a good shot of him."

We needn't have worried about being quiet, because our large friend wasn't going anywhere, except deeper into the alders. Patti came out with the camera, and we cautiously went up the driveway to the turnaround, as close as we could get. The big bull had lost his antlers and was nearly belly deep in the snow, enjoying the tasty ends of small twigs. But he was deep into an alder thicket, and a good photo was impossible.

"If I could get around to one side a bit," I thought out loud. Then I came up with the method. "I'll get the snowshoes," I announced. "Then walk around behind where he's standing and take photos."

We had been to the Hudson Bay Store in Thunder Bay a couple of weeks earlier and discovered their snowshoes were reasonably priced, so we had purchased a couple of pair of the traditional Chippewa models in the beavertail style. After coming home with the new snowshoes, we'd put on the bindings and tramped around in the foot or so of snow we'd had at the time. Now, I thought, the snowshoes would come into their own.

This is not the moose I saw while wearing snowshoes, but all the photos of that moose and others taken in the winter were so full of brush as to make the moose difficult to see.

"Be careful," Patti urged. "If he comes after you, you'll have to move fast."

"Don't worry," I said confidently. "This I can handle."

As soon as I stepped off the built-up snowbank onto the four feet of fluffy snow, I knew I was talking through my hat. The snowshoes went straight down nearly two feet, so I was standing more than knee deep in the snow. This was better than the vanishing Orange Julius but only narrowly. Each step had to be planned carefully and slowly taken.

Step by tedious step, I trudged through the snow in the planned direction. Soon I'd narrowed the sixty-foot distance to forty.

And then the moose stopped eating and turned to look seriously at me for the first time. I stood perfectly still.

"Oh, oh," Patti said needlessly.

The moose took a step, then another, squaring himself to me. At that moment I'd have given anything for a pair of wings.

Suddenly, the moose spun sideways as if to come around the alders toward me, and I turned to flee. One step, and I was on my face in the snow, thrashing forward in a strange emulation of the Australian crawl, snowshoes dragging at crazy angles from my feet. I fully expected flying hooves to stomp me flat at any moment.

When I somehow reached the plowed snowbank and was able to pull myself up, I had left both snowshoes behind and was on the last reserve of my strength.

"That's okay," Patti said calmly. "He went the other way."

I looked up, gasping for breath through the snow on my face, and saw the moose calmly feeding about twice as far away as he had been before.

"Jeez," I gasped, "God." I took two heaving breaths and shook my head, unable to get out a full thought. "Snowshoes . . . buried."

Somehow, I'd lost both snowshoes beneath the snow. The camera was covered with snow. It took several minutes of lying in the snow before I regained enough strength to pull myself up.

"I thought he was coming for me, for sure," I said. "Couldn't seem to move in that snow. Those snowshoes just got buried."

Patti sized me up and immediately repeated her assessment of a day earlier. "You look gray. I think you should go in and sit down. We'll get the snowshoes later."

I did as instructed, certain the "big one" was imminent, while Patti shot photos of the moose vaguely visible through a thick screen of alders. Those shots became the first of what we laughingly called our "moose in the bushes" photos. Over the years, it became a large collection because although these huge animals are easy to see, they are almost always standing behind something when they decide to stop and look at you.

* * *

Despite attempts to purchase everything needed for Christmas in our new "hometown" of Grand Marais, we needed some things we could only find in Duluth, one hundred five miles down the road. Some local businessmen make the drive every two or three days to pick up materials and supplies. We had not driven that far from home for several months, so it was an expedition as we set out on a day predicted to be free of new snow.

It was a cold, blustery day with tendrils of snow sweeping across the pavement. We were surprised at the amount of snow piled along the road in places like Schroeder, Beaver Bay, and Two Harbors. As we climbed the well-sanded Duluth hills toward the mall, seasonal decorations danced overhead in the gusty wind.

We had left in time to arrive at the Miller Hill Mall just as it opened, thinking that would allow us to beat the crowd. Hah! The parking lot was virtually full already, and as we drove slowly from row to row, people seemed to be staring at us. It made me feel uneasy.

"Why do I think people are looking at us so funny?" I asked. "Is there something wrong with us?" I could not imagine what it was. Our dirty white Jeep blended in perfectly.

"It's probably the Florida license plates," she said. "I think we have the only Florida tags in the entire city of Duluth."

"Could be," I muttered. "That's probably why people keep asking us when we're gonna leave for Florida. One day soon were going to have to get new plates, which means new driver's licenses. Then we'll be official residents."

"Yuck. I hate to take the test again," she said.

"Gonna have to if we're planning to stay here, which is what we've agreed on."

She nodded, unhappily. "It's hard to relocate."

We found a parking space about a block from where we entered the center. Walking past numerous cars, I noticed that every second or third car carried a warning flag or streamer of some bright color on the raised radio antenna, a precaution that reduced accidents when cars emerged from behind snowbanks at intersections. I hadn't seen such things since I was a kid, but then I hadn't seen this much snow since then, either.

We shopped quickly, stopped for a fast-food burger and fries on our way out of town and headed northeast. Snow flurries had been spitting all day and white plumes swirled as the car passed. The temperature outside had risen only into the single digits.

On our way to Duluth, we had seen a dozen deer alongside the road. Now we were seeing even more of the gray-brown white tails, their heavy winter coats ruffled by the wind.

We knew the deer herds gathered along the shore of Lake Superior every spring when motorists sometimes reported seeing a couple of hundred in two hours. But seeing so many of them in December was a surprise. We guessed the quantity of early snow had encouraged them to migrate earlier in the winter.

By the time we reached Cook County, still forty-five miles from home, we'd counted three dozen deer of assorted sizes. We came over a rise east of the Temperance River, now locked in winter's embrace, and saw what appeared to be a big, lanky dog run across the road ahead. I was just about to comment on the strangeness of seeing a dog out there at least a couple of miles from any house, when a second one crossed.

"Did you see that?" I asked.

"Wolves," Patti replied. "There goes a third one."

We watched as we closed the distance to the wolf crossing, where a fourth, fifth and sixth animal had run across at regular intervals, the final crossing made when we had closed to within less than a hundred yards. At the crossing point, we slowed to look down through the open woods of aspen and glimpsed two of the wolves before they slipped out of sight.

"Following the deer as they migrate down here to the warmer climate along the lake," I said.

"Sort of gives you the creeps, seeing all those wolves running right across the highway," Patti replied with a shudder. "Glad our little herd is still safe and sound around the house."

When we got home, nearly an inch of fresh snow had fallen on the driveway, filling the earlier tracks of the Jeep and of our resident deer. The tracks that had been fresh earlier in the day were the last we would see until spring. Our deer had migrated south.

❉ ❉ ❉

That night, after supper, Greg Olson pulled up to the house. I threw on a jacket and went out.

"Getting a lot of snow early this year," said the man who plowed our driveway, looking at the chest-high snowbanks. "Pretty soon I won't have any place to put it all, so I thought I'd bring the big Skip loader from the sawmill. It'll only take an hour or so to push some of the banks back."

"Whatever you think," I agreed.

"Well," he said. "If we don't push the banks back, I'm not gonna have room for the blade."

He pointed at the eight-foot-wide steel blade mounted at an angle on the front of his old Ford pickup, the bed of which was filled with frozen sand for extra traction when pushing a heavy load of snow.

I nodded in understanding. "Sure, do whatever you need to do."

"Yeah, well, I just wanted to get your okay."

I nodded again. He stood with his hand on the door, then looked up. "Your roof needs shoveling. Pretty heavy snow load."

I nodded without comment.

"So, how do you like it here? Getting along okay?" He asked.

"Yup. We really do like it."

"How'd you happen to come here, you know, come from Florida and pick this place?"

"Well, I've got lots of relatives here. You know the Backlunds? Rudy, John, Wes, Sid, Ted, Mike? All those guys?"

"Yeah, sure."

"Well, they're all my uncles and cousins. My name is spelled with an "e" instead of an "a." Got changed somewhere along the way, but we're all related."

"Well, I'll be darned." Greg said, his caution evaporating in a big grin. "That's pretty neat."

I returned his smile. "My grandad lived with old man Hedstrom when he came over from Sweden. That's before there was ever a sawmill over there. So we go way back." He nodded and smiled again, "I wondered why you moved up here. There's lots of people from the cities moving up here to live in the woods these days . . ."

He let the sentence hang, and I picked it up.

"So you probably do the plowing for some of them."

"Oh, yeah. Quite a few. Well, I gotta be going. I'll get the loader over here as soon as I can."

I waved goodbye as he turned the pickup around and drove away with taillights glowing red in the night.

I went in, took off my coat and fogged up glasses and recounted the conversation to Patti. Then I added a thought. "I think it makes people feel more secure, more relaxed maybe, if they can place you as part of a family. It's sort of like you belong, and didn't just wander up here by mistake."

"Family is great," Patti said thoughtfully. "It's made me feel at home here, a part of this place, even if it's an adopted family."

8

❄ Predators ❄

In the morning, I remembered what Greg Olson had said about the snow load on the roof, so I mentioned it to Patti.

"There's a story of that same thing in the local paper," Patti said. "Cabin owners who aren't here should arrange to have their roofs shoveled because of the heavy early snow."

I explained that I was going up to have a look, and she volunteered to come along. We ended up using two ladders to scale first the lower level then the upper roof, which was covered with knee-deep snow and needed clearing. Because of an aversion to heights, it was my first bird's-eye view from the second-story roof.

We made it up to the top ridge line and started shoveling while many of our bird visitors found perfect seats to watch us from the limbs of nearby trees.

In the current edition of the local weekly paper, there was a story about the annual December bird count, which had noted the ominous presence of Arctic birds not commonly found in northern Minnesota. Apparently, these birds, primarily the great gray owls and the snowy owls, ventured further south when food became scarce. Birders were warned to be on the alert since these raptors regularly staked out bird feeding stations as their food source.

So far we hadn't seen any of these arctic owls, but we had found, earlier that very morning, the remnants of a flying squirrel near our feeder.

These gentle creatures, which have the softest fur imaginable, would often visit our bird feeder after dark. We would sometimes hear them scamper across the roof, then fly down to a tree and across to the railing on the deck. We'd flip on the outdoor light and there they'd be, large, soft eyes looking out from where they huddled in the corner of the seed box.

We had heard and seen them regularly since summer, when they would sometimes arrive while we were still enjoying the twilight outside on the deck. But now a predator had also discovered them.

The next morning, a second partially eaten flyer was discovered by Patti on the deck.

"What could be doing this?" She asked sadly.

I shook my head, not knowing. "We'll just have to listen to the birds when they sound their warnings, then go out and have a look around. Eventually, we'll figure it out, assuming it's not happening in the middle of the night."

Since we were working at home all that day, we were able to hear the blue jays or the squirrels when they sounded their warnings. Then one of us would hurry to the back of the living room, look out the glass doors, then go outside.

All that day we monitored warning calls, but we couldn't tell what they were warning about. We saw nothing unusual.

"Well, this is getting us nowhere," I said.

"Have you got a better plan?" Patti asked.

"No, I guess not. It's just so frustrating."

She nodded in agreement, and we went back to our respective projects.

The warning sounded again.

"Right," I said in disgust since it was my turn, and I was getting tired of the silly jays and their warnings. They were like the boy who called "wolf" all the time.

I went to the back door and looked out, seeing nothing as expected. And then I saw it and involuntarily jumped back. Sitting not more than four feet above the feeder on a spruce branch, staring right through me with unblinking eyes, was the largest white owl I'd ever seen. Although I was only ten feet away, the owl acted like I wasn't even there.

I backed slowly away, then called upstairs to Patti. "Snooks, come here. The predator has arrived," I said tightly, trying to project my voice upstairs without frightening the big bird.

I needn't have worried. Patti hurried down, then went to the door and slowly slid it open. "Aren't you a handsome big fellow," she said to the owl, which sat silently.

She edged out and talked in a low voice to the owl, which looked at her with wide-eyed interest but did not move.

"I don't think he's afraid because he's probably never seen a person before," I suggested. "I wouldn't go much closer if I were you."

But my wife exhibits fearless behavior at the strangest times. Right then, she was advancing slowly while talking to the owl. When she was about six feet away, the big bird spread his wings to their full five-foot span and soared to another tree, where it again took up station.

"What do we do now?" Patti asked. "He's still going to hang around."

"And eat things," I added.

"And eat things," she agreed.

I shrugged, "Guess I'll scare it away. Maybe it won't come back."

I went out on the deck where the snow was moist enough to make marginal snowballs, and started throwing. After a couple of bad misses, I hit the tree above him, spattering him with snow, and he flew again, this time soaring far enough to be out of sight.

"What does such an owl eat?" Patti asked, so we adjourned to our copy of *Birds of North America*. It did not describe the snowy owl's diet, but it did inform us that the snowy's arctic pal, the great gray, ate rodents.

"Like mice," I said.

"Like squirrels, too," Patti added.

I nodded. Bertha and her gang were at risk, as well as the flyers. According to the bird book, these owls hunted night and day and had little fear of people.

But while we fretted over arctic owls, it was another predator that awakened us bolt upright from a deep sleep after midnight. A life-and-death battle was underway outside the house, and we jumped up to look down at the snarling and screaming shapes fighting in the moonlit snow.

A momentary look revealed a pine marten and a feral cat fighting in the snow, with the marten having the better of it. We slipped into robes and fleecy moosehide slippers and hurried downstairs, thinking that somehow, one of our cats had gotten out.

Out on the frozen deck, I jumped up and down and roared in my best imitation of King Kong, The marten broke off and fled across the sparkling blue snow while the cat, which was mostly yellow in color and not at all like any of ours, sat up and wondered what kind of animal he'd come up against.

In the light of morning, I went down for a look at the battlefield and found bits of yellow fur as well as a small opening into a cavity beneath the deck flooring. Apparently, the cat had hidden in the small cave and came out to attack what he thought was a smaller and weaker foe. His mistake almost cost him his life, and he moved on quickly to new quarters after the fight.

I often wondered through that winter how such animals as the lone cat survived. Perhaps he had caught the flying squirrels whose remnants we had discovered. Perhaps there was a mouse or two or an unwary squirrel, but life must have been hard and starvation close at hand for many such animals in the northern winter. No wonder the ravens stayed on a road kill even as a car passed close by on the highway. No wonder we saw fox tracks after every snowfall on our driveway, but only once saw an indication he'd ever found anything, in this case an unlucky partridge, to eat on our property.

We eventually saw the cat again, but the marten was soon back among the branches of the trees above the bird feeders on the back deck. I was on an errand to town when Patti stepped out on the deck in response to a blue jay alert.

At first she saw nothing, but the absence of birds and squirrels made her suspicious so she stayed out and looked around. It was then that she heard a rustling high in the tall poplar that stood sentinel over the corner of the deck.

She knew from experience it was a marten traveling quickly from limb to limb. But she could not possibly guess that it would advance, growling, as she yelled for it to go away. As it approached steadily down the trunk, she began to search for items on the deck she could throw. When her poor aim failed to discourage the marten, she picked up the snow shovel and swung it crashing against the deck railing. This move got his attention, and he stopped about ten feet overhead to reassess opportunity versus danger.

Another blow with the big metal shovel gave him reason to retreat, but not far, and the standoff began that continued for a half hour until I arrived home.

A pine marten seldom weighs as much as three pounds, though he appears bigger because of his long coat of rich brown fur. But he is a fearless character, single-minded in his focus on food. And when I got back, this particular marten was still awaiting the opportunity to eat something, preferably a squirrel or a bird.

"Hurry, hurry," Patti called from the deck as she saw me walk into the living room. "He won't leave and he almost got one of our squirrels," she stammered as I came outside. "He won't leave, and you've got to do something. One of Bertha's friends came toward the deck, and I tried to keep her away, and she kept coming." She gulped a breath and continued. "I thought he'd go after her and finally she got the message and took off across the snow. What will we do? You've got to scare him off. Don't kill him. Just get him to leave."

She pointed to a crotch about twenty feet up the tree where the marten, though partially hidden, was glaring down with yellow eyes. How to get him to leave but not kill him. The slingshot, which only stung the rump of a bear, would probably stop this small but nasty-tempered little guy for good.

"Well," I thought aloud, "guess that means a snowball attack."

"It won't hurt him?" Patti asked fearfully.

"Heck, I'll probably never hit him. I just hope he gets the message," I replied, kneading wet snow into a rough ball. I did not pack the snow hard on the long-shot chance that I might actually connect.

I threw, and the ball missed the tree completely. A second throw also missed. The third snowball hit above the marten, and he ducked as the snow flew. The fourth also missed, but the fifth hit close to the crotch, spraying the marten with snow chunks. He scrambled up the tree as I hollered and banged the shovel to keep him moving. High overhead, the tattletale blue jays set off their alarm cries as he went.

I tried one last snowball as he reached the canopy of the trees, but it fell short. But, once on the move, he seemed willing to keep going, and fairly flew through the interwoven branches sixty feet up. It was a good thing, too. My throwing arm felt as if it had been pulled from its socket.

A few trees over, the marten stopped and looked down. Patti was horrified he would stay. I waded through deep snow to the trunk of that particular tree and banged it hard with the shovel. Whether it was that noise or the vibration, Mister Marten resumed his journey across the forest roof. This time, he did not return for a while.

* * *

At the approach of Christmas, we had already settled into a wintertime routine, our activities ebbing and flowing with the weather conditions. When it was ten below zero, or when the snow was blowing, we stayed at home, entertaining ourselves wih cooking, music, reading, and epic games of Scrabble. Our radio picked up one station on a regular basis; fortunately it was a public radio station out of Houghton, Michigan, across Lake Superior. Television reception came from Duluth via a translator tower atop Sawtooth Mountain overlooking Grand Marais. Luckily, those of us on the back side of the tower also got good reception, so we had three network stations plus PBS. I will never forget our Saturday night television fare, an hour of Lawrence Welk reruns followed by Duluth Bulldog's hockey.

Christmas Eve morning dawned blustery and cold, but with a three-stop progressive dinner laid on, all concerns about the weather were put aside. We hosted the appetizer course, which included opening presents. Two of the teenagers arrived by snowmobile to put some adventure in the outing. Our second stop was at Gene and Linda Nelson's of Grand Marais, who were related by marriage. Gene had assembled a giant dining table from four-by-eight sheets of plywood to seat the big crowd for the traditional lutefisk dinner.

Now as anybody knows who comes from the Scandinavian parts of northern Minnesota, lutefisk carries with it a sniff of controversy. Not everyone finds it enticing. And the smell can be a bit bold. Some would call it rancid. It is, after all, soaked in lye. Thus it was that, halfway through the cooking, someone decided to throw open a window in the kitchen to air the place out. When we realized how cold the outdoor breeze was, it was already too late for several of Linda's carefully tended plants, which had been quick frozen.

Despite the mishap, all who wanted lutefisk had plenty before we moved on to a third stop at cousin Joan and Tim's house for dessert.

We got home at about eleven, and, before settling down with our presents to each other, we walked in the cold stillness down the driveway and looked up as the northern lights played among the stars. It had been an unusual but wonderful Christmas Eve with friends and relatives, and we clasped mittened hands as we walked with footsteps creaking over the hard-packed snow.

On Christmas morning, we got up and started work early to prepare for an afternoon family gathering that would go on until after dark. Just at dusk, the chorus of wolves gave a Christmas serenade, reminding everyone present that we were indeed close to the wilderness.

Yes, it really was that cold.

9

❄ A Person Could Die Out There ❄

If I were a snowbird, planning to spend the worst of winter in the sunny south, I'd stay in Minnesota until after Christmas, then pack the car and point it toward Florida, Texas, or Arizona. In fact, that is what many snowbirds do. They spend the holidays with family, get a solid helping of winter's delights, then bail out for the months of January, February, and March. And that is what many people, including relatives, thought we were planning to do.

So when New Year's Day came and went, and I pulled into Benson's gas station with the Jeep still bearing sunshiny Florida plates, he looked at me seriously and said, "I thought you'd be gone." After I gave him some foolishness about ice fishing and snowmobiling, he shook his head. "If I were you," he replied," I would be in Florida by now." Then he shrugged and rang up the twenty-dollar gas purchase.

After New Year's Day, the real northern winter sets in, all that came before having been a pleasant rehearsal. That's what the locals like to say. The sun slides low across the southern tree tops, whose branches clatter in a frozen windy dance. Even when the temperature climbs desperately above the zero mark, the wind chill doesn't.

I know it gets colder for longer periods in places like Nome, Alaska, or Yellowknife, in Canada's Northwest Territories. But not many people have ever experienced that. Probably not more than one percent of North America's population have ever seen temperatures of forty-five below zero, not counting wind chill, or have seen solid ice on the lakes in mid-May. But it can happen here in the course of a winter, and it explains why rural folks were cutting and splitting wood in the warmth of summer, just to be prepared.

Of course this nearly perpetual cold occasionally breaks, and when the mercury does climb unexpectedly and amazingly into the thirties, one can expect to see a convertible with the top down or the UPS man delivering packages in his shorts. It happens.

So here it was January and the last of the part-timers had slipped away. We were down to the hard core. I suppose it was only fitting that the first outing of the new year should involve ice fishing and snowmobiles and cold weather.

Hal, who worked at the newspaper said he'd pick me up Saturday morning at 7:00 A.M., and we'd head for Saganaga to catch some lake trout. Having heard a lifetime of big fish stories about Saganaga, and having sampled its open water fishing myself, I accepted eagerly.

When he arrived in the dimness of dawn and we loaded my snowmobile aboard his double trailer alongside his own, I knew it was cold. "How cold?" I asked.

He shrugged. "Not too bad." About minus five at his house in town, he said. With that reassurance, I didn't bother checking the thermometer but loaded my gear aboard, and we headed north on the Gunflint Trail.

To reach Saganaga Lake, or Sag as it is called, involves a sixty-mile car trip over snow-packed roads, followed by about ten miles on a snowmobile. Then fishermen and women stand out on the open ice like demented Siberian refugees, hoping the fish will bite.

When we arrived at the Sag landing, two other parties were unloading their snow machines. From the amount of steam rising as they went about their preparations to leave,

I could tell it was cold. Very cold. The inside of my nose confirmed this; at first breath it felt instantly frozen.

"A bit nippy out here," I mentioned in casual understatement to two men checking the bungee cords on their loads.

"Nippy, hell," one responded as he turned toward me to reveal an already frosted beard. "My thermometer shows thirty-eight below."

"Oh yeah? Well, I suppose it could be about that."

He continued to organize gear, so I said nothing further. We were apparently going fishing.

After traveling a couple of miles I called a halt. The visor on my helmet had frozen over. I pulled my hand from the chopper and liner and tried to clear it, without luck. So I lifted it and drove on with my face exposed to the wind.

That was even worse. In a mile or so, my face was numb and so was my hand pressing down the accelerator. I stopped again, this time managing to set the visor low enough to reduce the wind but high enough to see under. I put my numb fingers inside my snowmobile suit against the skin to bring them around. By then Hal, who hadn't looked back the second time, was just a dot a mile ahead.

As a kid growing up in northern Minnesota, I'd never had trouble with frozen hands when wearing the traditional chopper mitts and wool liners. Must be bad circulation, I thought. This time when I set off, I alternated hands on the throttle, first right, then left. It was clumsy but the only way to keep my fingers from freezing solid.

After traveling six or seven miles, Hal stopped, and I caught up. Neither hand had much feeling now, but I didn't mention it.

"I'll go on ahead," he said, "and you take it slow. We're about halfway."

"Where did those other guys at the landing go?" I asked.

"You'll see them up ahead, parked the same place we'll park." He dropped his visor and set off again, quickly accelerating so that his machine disappeared in a cloud of flying snow.

I followed much more slowly, switching hands every half minute or so to keep the fingers from freezing. After about twenty minutes, I saw the small pack of sleds parked ahead and drove toward them, where I found Hal standing alone next to his Polaris.

I was about to ask where everybody had gone when he explained that we were now in Canada and would leave our snowmobiles and walk back into Minnesota. The Minnesota side was part of the Boundary Waters Canoe Wilderness Area, and no snowmobiles were allowed there. So having arrived in Canada, we would now walk half a mile back to commence fishing. As we set off carrying our gear, I could see tiny black spots on the ice ahead.

As much as I dreaded the long walk, it did me good, and by the time we arrived, I could even notice feeling in my nose. We wore ourselves out drilling four holes with a hand augur through eighteen-inch ice, then baited up and commenced waiting. Minute by minute, the cold came back, seeping through unseen places until I was marching in place to keep warm. I didn't even care if I was scaring the fish below. A person could freeze to death out here, I thought to myself.

This went on about four hours, until Hal finally felt we had done enough penance on the ice to merit a trip back home. By then, the others had left empty handed. I wish I could say we caught a fish, but we didn't.

It was four in the afternoon when we got home and I horsed the snowmobile off Hal's trailer. I went inside, told Patti what had happened, sat down in front of the crackling fireplace and fell asleep until suppertime.

I don't know what it is about ice fishing that hooks some people like overgrown bass. A week later, cousin Mike and his wife, Nancy, said they'd meet us up in Magnetic Bay just off Gunflint Lake. Mike said he knew "the spot," and I believed him.

Patti and I pulled out of our driveway at dawn, towing the snowmobile, and arrived at Gunflint Lake an hour later. It was a sunny day but there was a ground blizzard underway, and visibility was almost nil on the lake. We found Mike's empty pickup in the lot and assumed they had set out to cross the big lake with or without visibility.

"What do you think?" Patti asked.

"I think we better take a rough compass heading across to Magnetic Bay and try to travel that course," I said.

We set out just west of north and ran about twenty miles per hour through the blowing snow. I figured we'd strike the shoreline just west of where Gunflint ran into Magnetic Bay. As we neared the wooded shoreline, the wind eased, and we could suddenly see exactly where we were. I am forever glad we didn't aim for the opening between the two bodies of water because we saw open water in the middle of the narrows. The current from Gunflint to Magnetic had kept the ice from forming there.

We carefully edged around the point on good ice and then stopped to scan the surface of the bay. Far to the north, at the base of a cliff, we could make out a couple of dots on the ice, so we set out toward them. It was Mike and Nancy and their golden retriever Boomer, already set up and fishing.

We pulled up to the shoreline out of the wind and kicked open a couple of old lightly frozen over holes. The temperature was about zero, quite comfortable in the quiet sunshine.

Mike lit a fire using dead branches from a blown down birch, and we enjoyed fresh grilled hot dogs while waiting for our fish to bite. All too soon the hot dogs were gone, and we were still awaiting the fish. We tried different jigs and different holes. Still no bites. After four hours of inaction, I said we had to go to get back for a church meeting we'd promised to attend. I had had it with ice fishing, a feeling shared completely by Patti.

The next day, Patti called Nancy to find out how they had done after we left.

"So what happened?" I asked.

"They stayed another four hours," she said, "and they didn't get a bite

I shook my head. Patti and I were not, and would never be, that fond of ice fishing. "Promise me something," I said to her. "Promise that you will not let us go ice fishing for at least a month."

"Do you really mean that?" She asked.

"Yes, I really do," I answered truthfully.

"Good," she said. "There's something I'd much rather do, anyway."

I hardly dared ask what she had in mind. She told me anyway.

"The Beargrease Race starts today," she said. "I want to watch some of the sled dog teams."

"Great. Let me sit down and study the section in today's paper so we'll know when they're coming."

For many years, city fathers and would-be promoters in northern climes have attempted to plumb the depths of winter for sources of revenue. Inevitably, they conjure up a race or a tournament or a festival. Thus, there are broomball tournaments, curling bonspiels, snowmobile races, snowshoe competitions, and sled dog races.

The one-thousand-mile Iditarod in Alaska is sled dog racing's premier event. Not far behind at that time was the John Beargrease Marathon, named for a sled-dog-driving Chippewa mail carrier, which ran from Duluth to Grand Portage and back, a distance of about five to six hundred miles. With a large enough purse to attract some of the top Alaskan drivers and other notables, the Beargrease was a five- or six-day sprint, with about eighty-five hours of racing and another thirty or so of mandatory rest. The curious twist to both Iditarod and Beargrease races is that some of featured stars have been and are women.

I always thought that sled dogs were those big, furry "huskies" we associate with Alaska and Eskimos. Those dogs are tough and durable, but they're much too big and slow for racing. Instead, the racers have bred a smaller, thinner dog, which might be most any color and who knows what mixture of breeds.

The teams started coming through on Tuesday just before dawn. We went over to Skyport Lodge and waited for the leaders to come from the west down Devil's Track Lake, which runs seven miles west to east.

It was fifteen below and windless, the smoke from Skyport's old pot-bellied stove rising in a straight column against the rose-edged sky.

"There she comes," someone said, pointing west across the dimly lit ice. A murmur went up from the twenty or so hardies who waited with us. Soon others pulled themselves from the wood stove's warmth to come out into the cold.

"I see her," Patti said, and sighted down her arm to give me an idea of the musher and team's exact location.

The crowd watched in silence as the dark dot lengthened and became eighteen dogs and a sled driven by Dee Dee Jonrowe from someplace called Willow, Alaska.

As I watched the dogs come across the ice, silken and silent and much faster than I had expected, my eyes filled with tears that spilled onto my glasses and froze. Those dogs did not run so much as they flowed like well-oiled machines, and the idea that one small woman had taken them alone through the wilderness, moving night and day, was more than my senses could absorb.

They came up off the ice, hung a right behind the lodge, and Jonrowe brought the dogs to a stop next to a line of hay bales. We watched as she and two handlers fed the dogs and bedded them down in the hay. She talked to each dog and gave it real attention before going on to the next. Only after seeing to all the dogs did she go into the lodge and have a cup of coffee while doing radio interviews. Then, within an hour, before the second team came into sight across the ice, she and her team were off into the sunrise, sled runners hissing on the snow, destined for the turnaound sixty miles ahead at Grand Portage.

The second and third place teams emerged onto the sunlit ice within sight of each other. Nearing the lodge, team two took a slightly different path, just a hundred feet from Jonrowe's, and came to a halt.

We watched, not understanding what had happened, until someone with binoculars said, "Oh, my God, they're in the water."

Sometimes, when heavy snow covers the ice, the weight of it causes sections of the lake to flood right over the ice. The snow covering might appear perfectly dry, but just beneath it may lie a two- or three-foot layer of mushy snow and water on top of the ice. This is virtually guaranteed to mire down a snowmobile or a sled-dog team.

So the second-place team was struggling in this dangerous freezing mush as the third-place team approached. Seeing the trouble, the musher circled wide around the flooded area, then halted and anchored his team. He ran back to the lead dog of the mired team and the two mushers, working knee deep in slush, led the lead dog through the freezing mixture and back onto the hard-packed snow.

It was an amazing display of courage and sportsmanship, and we were still talking about it a half hour later when we

Musher emerging from the snow in the John Beargrease sled race.

reached the Greenwood Road and turned east off the Gunflint Trail so as to get another glimpse of the woman leading the race. We climbed up on the six-foot ridge of snow along the plowed road just where she would hang a ninety-degree right onto a narrow trail that led into the woods toward Grand Portage. A small sign with a red arrow showed the right turn.

We waited only a couple of minutes before her team came into sight on the Greenwood Road, moving swifty and silently in that long-legged trot that ate the miles. The dogs wore wool booties, so the silence was broken only by the hiss of the sled and her call of "Gee, Gee" as she neared.

The lead dog spotted the opening in the snowbank and turned right with the team snaking behind him. In seconds, the entire assemblage was lost in the snow-covered spruce and pine.

I know it sounds simplistic to talk of the beauty and grace that can be achieved by a sled-dog team moving across a snowscape. There is a peace and fluidity that resembles few other things I've seen.

And yet, just below that level of skill and understanding, a dozen or more sled dogs can create some of the God-awfulest tangles and chaos imaginable when they get confused or excited. We saw this for ourselves during the start of the Beargrease in downtown Grand Marais. One team found itself tangled up in the middle of the grocery store parking lot. Another set out up the highway. The enthusiasm of the dogs at the start of a race is such that the musher carries an extra passenger or drags a tire to slow them down.

Cook County, because of its elbow room and remote location, offers a "perfect setting" for mushers to live with and train their dogs. A number of local sled-dog handlers have become racers, breeders, tour operators, and arctic explorers. The staging adjacent to the non-motorized wilderness area and the long season of snow are ideal components in the making of sled dog enthusiasts.

Experience in handling long, cold winters also is a commodity that endears local residents to those employers looking to fill Antarctic jobs. A number of locals have successfully handled the Antarctic winter and return each year for more.

Confused chipmunk in the snow. "Hey, you're supposed to be asleep."

10

❊ Explorations ❊

As we slid into deep winter, we fell into a routine that seemed to work. Patti got up about six or six thirty, wrapped herself in a shawl or blanket and wrote devotions for an hour or so. About an hour later, I climbed out of bed, threw on a sweatsuit and Sorels and descended into the furnace room beneath the garage to light the heating system. Meanwhile, Patti put out seeds for our growing flock of birds.

If fresh snow had fallen, we would then shovel the front walk and the back deck, play with Bertha a couple of minutes and go in for our usually brief planning session to decide on an outing for the afternoon and menu for that night.

Then I went up to the spare bedroom overlooking the driveway and garden and settled down for two or three hours of writing. I was working on a mystery novel that would eventually become *Golden Fleece*, published in 1990. Patti used this time to clean and cook and generally handle the management of the household.

After lunch, I'd check the chip burner and feeder system again, then we'd be off for two or three hours on our daily "outing." As we had observed earlier in the winter, some residents went into a sort of hibernation during the coldest times and became couch potatoes and TV zombies. If we could get out for two to three hours each afternoon, even if it was for grocery shopping or a long ride through the forest on the back roads via Jeep or snowmobile, we could avoid the ultimate boredom of doing nothing.

Then, by 4:00 P.M. as darkness followed the sun across the sky, we would be back home, checking the furnace. We ate supper early, watching the news, then caught a TV show or two or played Scrabble before going upstairs to read and listen to music, usually a set of several tapes that featured piano classics, or perhaps some music on the Minnesota Public Radio programming carried by the Houghton station.

In this routine, excitement often took the form of an unusual bird at the feeder, strange tracks on the driveway or perhaps a moose rump-deep in the snowy hazel brush.

Ever since late summer, we had been accumulating a flock of evening grosbeaks. This was a raucous crowd, descending three dozen strong on the feeders and frightening other birds out of their way. Many were juveniles, born in our woods and unwilling to leave the only home they'd known.

In mid-December, the green horde had been joined by a pair of red pine grosbeaks. Next time we noticed, there were a half-dozen of these beautiful birds whose quiet demeanor was such a contrast to their bossy crowd of green cousins.

January also saw the start of squirrel mating season. At first, this consisted of male squirrels trying to hang around the back deck and Bertha chasing them away. As the days passed, the boys were more determined to stay around, and Bertha more certain than ever that they must be sent packing. This led to some of the greatest aerobatic chases imaginable through the treetops. Although she always seemed to return victorious, the effort was taking its toll on the queen of the deck, and she sometimes stretched out for a nap before resuming her activities.

When Bertha was on the deck, Patti would often set a few nuts out for her. Unlike the chipmunks, she could only carry

One of the red squirrels on the deck.

one at a time, so she'd grab it and set off across the snow drifts for the garage. It could take her ten minutes to haul three nuts to her current hiding place, and in that time, the crafty bluejays would figure out what was going on and quickly descend to haul off the remaining nuts.

At first, we didn't understand how the nuts were disappearing so quickly, then Patti saw a bluejay fly in and caught on. After that, she'd set out only two or three nuts for Bertha.

The one thing that made this little red squirrel so dear to our hearts was the fact she would come when called. Patti would sit on the deck calling, "Bertha, Bertha," and here would come a small red shape racing across the snow to be at her side.

Sometimes, Bertha would eat sunflower seeds when we were outside with her; other times she'd stretch out in the sun for a snooze. We never saw another red squirrel do this. Then there were times for fun and games, when Patti would hide a nut in the fold of her sweater, and Bertha would climb all over her looking for it.

More often than not, our back deck sessions would draw an interested and ever-hungry observer, Poe, the raven. As he understood more about Patti and the scraps she saved for him, he would fly over and call attention to himself, sqawking that hoarse, guttural "caw caw" that is lower in pitch and less melodic than the similar call made by crows.

His verbal reminder often worked. Hearing Poe's call, Patti would say, "Oh, my gosh, that reminds me. I've got scraps left over from making the hot dish, and I saved them for Poe and his mate." Off she'd go to the kitchen and then down the driveway to the big poplar where Poe landed to wait. By the time she got back to the house, Poe had dropped down to the snow, picked up a prize morsel and flown off through the woods to find his mate.

Despite our plan to avoid ice fishing, our daily outings often took that form. There were always stories circulating down at the gas station or grocery store or church, just about anywhere I ran into one of those dyed-in-the-wool ice fishermen. I couldn't resist them. The conversations went like this:

"Hey, you been out ice fishing?"

"No, how 'bout you?"

"Not so much. Been busy, but I heard they're biting up on Loon. So and so got their limit, and one went twenty pounds."

"Oh really? Where do they fish? That's a big lake to just go up there blind."

"Easy to find the spot. Go east from the landing a half mile and fish the plateau. About forty feet. You'll see all the holes."

Armed with such sure-fire information, I'd approach Patti on the subject.

"Sounds like an easy place to get to, and the fish are biting," I'd say.

"Sure, let's give it a try," she'd say, and off we'd go to Loon Lake with the minnows, ice fishing equipment, and snowmobile.

We did not catch a trout at Loon Lake, but we got a couple of bites, which primed us for the next fish story we heard.

"Did you hear about the walleyes they're getting up at South Fowl?"

So off we'd go to South Fowl—sixty miles of driving followed by several miles of snowmobile travel, to stand in the blowing snow in the vain hope a walleye would bite.

Fueled by such fish stories, we made trips to Birch, Clearwater, and Mayhew in search of lake trout, and Mink, Musquash, and Trestle Pine for splake, which are a cross between speckled trout and lake trout. In no case did we catch more than a single fish.

Because we fished on weekdays, we rarely saw a soul. We did see where others had been fishing. We even saw where they had caught fish. But when we were there, the fish did not bite.

One blustery day, as we sat out on the ice at Trestle Pine, two men walked toward us across the lake. They were obscured partially by the blowing snow. One was pulling a large sled, while the other carried a packsack.

They passed close to us, and we waved at each other, then they kept going toward the far shore, where they went into the woods and disappeared. I knew from the map that the trail led to another lake, which then had to be nearly traversed to reach the area of good fishing. They would have walked at least two miles before they could set up shop.

Patti and I watched them go and agreed that what we were doing was crazy. It made no sense to go traipsing after every fish story we heard. Heck, neither of us even liked to ice fish.

So we halted the fishing forays and used our afternoons to explore the countryside more thoroughly. Instead of staring at a bobber in a freezing hole in the ice, or the flag of a tip-up device, we started learning more about the travel habits of the wild animals that lived around us. What we learned made perfect sense, even if it disagreed with what some of the conservationists said.

Their arguments against roads went something like this: "If a road is built through wolf or bear or moose range, it will reduce their range because the animals will drift back in the woods a certain distance, say three-fourhs of a mile for wolves, to escape the sound of cars. The road thus reduces the range by a mile and a half times the length of the road. With a twenty-mile road, it effectively reduces a wolf's range by thirty square miles." At least that's the essential theory I've heard and read, with distance variable for different animals.

What a whopper! I'd like to take that theorist along on a ride through the back country of northeastern Minnesota where these wild animals use the same roads we do for travel because it's easier than mucking about in waist-deep snow.

And winter habits apparently carry over to other seasons, as well. Even without snow, you'll find the moose or bear traveling the back roads because it's easier and it takes him where he wants to go.

Many times, a road cuts across a well-traveled animal track. Does the animal abandon the trail because of the road? Of course not. He simply crosses the road when he encounters it.

So, many afternoons we'd simply pick a road, plowed or unplowed, and take either Jeep or Ski Doo for a trip along its length. Most times when we saw tracks in fresh snow, we'd stop for a closer look. Carrying a track identificaion book, we came, through practice, to know many wild animal prints and speculate on some we didn't know.

The tracks often told stories. A moose followed by three wolves, big ones judging from their saucer-size prints. A lynx or bobcat waiting at the edge of a hazelbrush patch full of snowshoe hare prints. More often an animal traveled alone, stopping to look and listen and perhaps nibble a few bites, then resuming its journey.

The woods are quiet this time of year. It's easy to figure out why when you think of the many species that hibernate: bears, raccoons, skunks, frogs, chipmunks, groundhogs. And migrating birds are also gone. Hawks, geese, ducks, other waterfowl, robins and other songbirds, woodcock. We gain a few birds from further north, but not many.

Then of course, the deer, which spread out through the woods in summer, have migrated toward the moderating weather influence of Lake Superior, followed closely by many of the area's wolves and coyotes.

So we sometimes traveled a few blocks seeing only the fresh carpet of white before we saw a track, but the trip was still eventful. In places where the moose were plentiful, they would track up an acre or more, just milling around in their search for something good or at least nourishing to eat. Mostly they chewed the tender ends of branches like moose willow.

In contrast to this widespread use of the back country roads by wild animals, we sometimes traveled long distances through the woods without seeing the tracks of any major animal. White, undisturbed snow lay deep in the woods in January, and animals avoided it. Travel patterns only changed later in the winter, when the freezing and thawing cycle began, and hard crusts atop the snow allowed many predators—foxes, wolves, and coyotes—to stay on top, while the moose and deer with their sharp hooves broke through.

On one of our afternoon drives, we traveled up the Gunflint Trail and passed close to Mayhew Lake, where we had recently fished for lake trout. As we passed, the wind was blowing snow across the ice in a scene that could have been arctic in origin. Then, during a lull between gusts, we caught a glimpse of two parka-clad figures sitting on five-gallon plastic buckets, backs to the wind, staring down at their bobbers. "What an awful way to spend an afternoon," Patti said.

"My thoughts exactly," I agreed. "I'd much rather pay $4.95 for salmon fillets at the store and spend the afternoon doing something else."

We climbed the hill past the two fishermen and started down the steep grade when I suddenly saw the big moose step out into the road. Driving on hard-packed snow, this is one of winter's most frightening moments. If I hit the brakes too hard, I'd lose control and start sliding. Too little braking and I'd hurtle down the hill into the moose at nearly full speed.

Somehow, at that moment, I remembered the horn, which I blew steadily as we neared the thousand-pound impediment. At the last moment, he moved one step back, and we slipped past, still doing thirty.

Phil Hedstrom told us a similar moose story one day while riding the Gunflint further south.

"Years ago, before we had seat belts, I came over Northern Light Hill, and there were two moose standing right in the road below me," he said. "I hit the brakes, closed my eyes and hung on. Somehow, those moose separated just enough to let me slide on by. Otherwise, I'd have been down in the river."

Just a couple of weeks before our near miss, Justine Kerfoot described a moose collision in her local newspaper column. It was night, and she was returning home to Gunflint Lake when the moose suddenly appeared in her windshield, literally. She hit the moose, and his head left an imprint in her windshield. After she stopped, she got out, uninjured, expected to see a dead or injured animal. Instead, she only saw where the tracks disappeared into the woods. Next morning, she brought her son Bruce and a couple of others, including a forest ranger, to look for the moose, but it had kept on running. Imagine hitting a moose in the head hard enough to leave his imprint on your windshield and having him walk away. Amazing.

We came home late that afternoon, just before dark, to find a pile of feathers in the snow below the deck. The prints in the snow told a story of the partridge being hit by a predator, which had leaped from behind a small spruce tree. We could actually see where the animal had attacked him.

The predator had picked out the partridge feathers and then either eaten the bird or carried it off toward a snow-covered blowdown near the creek. As our eyes followed the trail of blood and feathers down the hill, something moved.

"There, right by the blowdown. What is it?" Patti asked.

I watched as a large, weasel-like animal with dark brown fur grabbed what little of the partridge remained and carried it out of sight into the snow. The animal, which was twice or three times the size of a marten but similar in shape, appeared to have found a snow cave in the blowdown. "Fisher," I said. "That's what it is. We must have interrupted his dinner."

"Oh, my gosh. You don't suppose that was Percy?" Patti clapped her head over her mouth in horror at the thought of a dire end to our favorite partridge.

"No, we've never seen him in back, only in front. There have been other partridges around, but they stay back here. Percy's taken over the feeder in the cherry tree. I'm sure it's not him."

Neither Patti or I had ever seen a fisher, though I'd seen a couple of pelts purported to be fisher. This animal appeared to be about two feet long, followed by a lush tail of almost equal length. Taken as a whole, the fisher appeared dangerous and unafraid, and I certainly had no plans to reconnoiter the snow-covered brush pile in which it was hiding.

Dusk was coming on fast, and later that evening, when we threw a flashlight beam at the pile, we saw a trail leading away from the snowy den. The fisher was gone, and we never saw it return.

The next morning, we checked our inventory of birds and animals. Bertha arrived early and was fine. The collection of chicadees, nuthatches, blue jays, and grosbeaks were all accounted for. The woodpeckers out front were swinging merrily on their net-encased suet slabs, and by noon, we even logged in the return of our favorite front-yard partridge, Percy. Poe circled overhead, and Patti declared the grounds safe once more. The fisher was gone, and we never saw it again, even though its lone foray into our back yard had provided good hunting.

Chickadee taking wing from the suet ball.

11

❄ Real Minnesotans ❄

Having committed ourselves to the full northern winter, it began to seem obvious that we would have to make other residency commitments, as well. So, one day, I stopped at the court house to pick up a driver's information book.

Back home, I announced that we were going to get Minnesota driver's licenses.

"No," was Patti's response.

"No?" I asked, surprised.

"I'm not going to do it. I'll never be able to park between those flags. That street is just ice and snow."

I explained to her that no driving would be involved, just a written test that we'd study for by reading the booklet I'd brought home.

"You're certain?" She said.

"Absolutely. No question."

"Well, I'm not taking a driver's test, and that's final. I've been looking at those black pylons with red flags on top all winter, and the more I look, the more I've dreaded taking a test. There's no way I could park there and that means no test."

"Well, you don't have to worry. We'll study together and ace the questions. Then we'll have new driver's licenses. We'll get Minnesota tags and new auto insurance. That makes us Minnesotans for sure. That's what we want to be, right?"

She nodded. "Right, but no driver's test."

"Right," I agreed.

Two days later, we passed the test and became official Minnesota residents. It was a cold day but there was sun, and as I squatted in front of the Jeep to attach the new "Land of 10,000 Lakes" plates, I swear I could feel a bit of warmth from the white orb in the southern sky. Almost a month had passed since the equinox in December, and although the sun still hung low, the days were already growing a bit longer and brighter.

A certain sign of this was the length of icicles at the eaves. As the snow began to melt on south-facing roofs, the icicles grew larger. And the ice on the edge of the roof began to thicken. When this buildup occurs, it's called an ice dam. It was a portent of trouble to come, but we didn't know enough to worry about it yet.

A curious thing happened when we officially became Minnesotans; like other Minnesotans we started thinking about going south for a vacation. Or at least I did.

"I don't need to go to Florida," Patti said. "I just came from there."

Rebuffed, I quietly thought about a good time and place to go. Late February seemed right, because when we got back two weeks later, it would be warmer and, perhaps, less snowy. How could I have forgotten that March is the snowiest month of the winter? Most of the really bad blizzards came in March.

For the moment, I said nothing of my thoughts. Having planted the idea in Patti's mind, I would wait and see if it took root.

❆ ❆ ❆

At the wood chip mine, where we toiled every third day, we had reached the front of the trailer, then removed the "roof" of ice-bound chips, and were now working toward the edges. At this pace, we'd be out of chips in six weeks and ready for another load from the mill.

The sound of "Keee-Keee" ringing clear in the air caused us both to stop and look up at the blue sky overhead.

"There" Patti said, pointing almost into the sun. I shielded my eyes and scanned until I picked up the soaring hawk, our first in about three months.

"I knew it sounded like the hawks around in the summer," I said, watching the bird do graceful loops. A second series of "Keee-Keee-Keee" broke the cold silence, and we spun around to watch a second hawk soar into view over the treetops. They were hunting together, just like the pair of hawks we'd come to know in the summer and who lived close to the ravens in our woods.

A squirrel sounded a call of alarm, and we smiled. "Well, at least Bertha is aware of the danger and is telling her friends," I said. "Maybe those hawks are just passing through. If so, they'll be hunting a mile from here in just a few minutes."

We continued to watch the hawks as Bertha chattered another warning, this time closer to the house.

"Oh, dear," Patti fretted. "I hope she doesn't run out on the railing and just stand there in plain sight."

"Surely she's got more sense than that," I said hopefully.

Patti walked to the back end of the trailer where she could see out to the yard and the steep A-frame roof.

Bertha came into view, and, at first, Patti smiled. "There you are, Bertha," she exclaimed.

Bertha stopped to look at us waving to her from the trailer, then looked up as another set of "Kees" echoed across the sky.

And then she shocked us completely. Before the final cry from the hawk had died out, she was on her way up the steep roof. As Bertha reached the ridgeline, Patti said, a quiet, "Oh, my God," then followed that with a loud directive, "Bertha, you get down from there this minute!"

The squirrel responded by running right to the end of the ridgeline and standing defiantly, chattering up at the intruding hawks. She looked like a figurehead at the prow of a ship. Patti was terrified now for her little friend.

"Bertha. Come on, Bertha," she yelled, then muttered a prayer and shouted another warning.

Meanwhile, the two hawks continued to circle, no doubt amazed or at least confused by this little red squirrel's show of bravery. Our flock of song birds had long since flown to the cover of nearby trees, and only Bertha challenged the raptors.

This went on for at least five minutes—seeming more like an hour—as the hawks keed and the squirrel chattered angrily and we yelled until we were hoarse and waved our arms.

Then, as quickly as she had scaled the roof, Bertha scooted down at an angle, jumped to a large snow drift and ran over to the trailer.

"You foolish, foolish squirrel," Patti said gently, giving our protector a nut to reward her glory. "Don't you know enough to be afraid of those hawks?"

Bertha took her nut gently, positioned it in her mouth, then turned and bounded gracefully across the snow into the forest tangle. We shook our heads and glanced up one more time to find the sky empty, the hawks gone.

I shook my head. Bertha, queen of the back deck, had done it again, vanquished the intruders, with an aggressiveness that had confounded her adversaries.

We went back to shoveling and prying the icy chips, replaying in words what had gone through our minds during Bertha's challenge. Fear, frustration, amazement, anger, and finally relief. What a spectrum of emotions flooded out during the little squirrel's rooftop stand. It was something we would not soon forget. The legend of Bertha was growing.

That evening we tuned in the weather from Duluth to hear the ecstatic forecaster predicting a heat wave. Thanks to a rare combination of air moving north from the Gulf of Mexico, we would be included in a thin band of warm air that would send our thermometer soaring into the forties.

"I'll believe it when I see the snow melting," Patti said doubtfully.

"We should plan something fun to do tomorrow afternoon, just in case," I suggested. "How about a long snowmobile ride over to Devil's Track Lake and then north on the Gunflint snowmobile trail? We could ride all the way to Poplar Lake and back."

"If it's forty degrees, I'll do it," Patti agreed.

During the night the thermometer obeyed predictions and climbed steadily. In the morning, it was above the freezing mark. For the first time in weeks, I felt caged in my writing room, jumping up at every sound to see what was happening. Patti came in at 11:00 A.M.

"Getting anything done?" She asked, knowing full well that I was not able to concentrate.

"What's the temperature?" I replied.

"Over forty and sunny," she grinned. "You get the snowmobile ready, and I'll make us sandwiches to eat on the trail."

"It's a deal," I agreed, jumping out of my old office chair.

Forty degrees may not seem like anybody's idea of warmth, but we were accustomed to zero and below; it felt positively balmy. Two mornings earlier, the thermometer had read minus twenty-five degrees; if the day warmed to forty-five, that would be a difference of seventy degrees.

Dressed in our usual snowmobile suits, we set off down the back roads to reach the state trail, then followed it to where the northbound trail intersected. That took us out onto the ice of Devil's Track Lake, and we rode west about five miles to the summer campground, where we followed the trail north into the woods. Finding a quiet, sunny spot protected from the south wind by a cluster of spruce trees, we stopped for lunch. The warmth was positively glorious, well into the fifties in the sun.

We unzipped our snowmobile suits, took off helmets and gloves and enjoyed Patti's pastrami and rye with a side offering of dill pickles.

"With this, I can survive the winter," I laughed. "With this I can get by without a vacation."

"It's wonderful," Patti echoed, her face angled toward the sun with eyes closed.

All this enjoyment, and we didn't have to worry about the chip burner. It had been so warm in the house before we'd left that I shut down the system. We'd let the sun provide heat as it poured through the big living room windows.

After half an hour in the sun, we set off north, once passing over a small bridge that spanned a small open creek whose black water proved a surprising contrast to the otherwise white world. It must have been kept open by warm springs, a rarity in the area.

We traveled another dozen miles to where the trail crossed the South Brule on the old highway bridge, then stopped within earshot of the Gunflint Trail. Just two weeks earlier, we'd watched Dee Dee Jonrowe traverse this same section of trail on her way to victory in the Beargrease Marathon. That day had been below zero; today was fifty degrees warmer and the snow wet and tacky.

Just past the bridge, we turned the snowmobile around and started back, up the steep hill and onto the narrow forest trail. With my face mask pushed up and my heavy mitts put away, I felt more in tune with Orange Julius than ever. As for Patti, riding behind me, her sense of balance was amazing, honed by motorcycle riding in earlier years.

We came to the shore of Devil's Track Lake and turned east, down the lake.

"Faster," Patti shouted over the roar of the air-cooled engine.

I grinned. From our first ice-fishing trip, she had been afraid of travel over frozen lakes. Her theory was that speed would take us across the bad places before we fell through into the water. I thought about it and smiled again, realizing she might have been right.

I tightened my grip on the throttle, and we sped up to forty miles per hour on the flat surface. Top speed for the Tundra was about forty-five, which felt like seventy to me, but was snail-like compared to most sleds, which could run at sixty miles per hour or even eighty across the open ice.

At forty, I felt we were just at the edge of control, but Patti was much more relaxed and riding easily. For her, speed was the safety margin.

We got home just after the sun had disappeared into the western treeline, and the temperature had cooled noticeably.

Ramah met us stiffly at the door.

"What's wrong, old girl?" I asked, giving her a few strokes behind the ears. She had been stiffening noticeably of late, unable to run and walking with a limp. At first we'd thought it was some kind of arthritis brought on by the cold. But now, we weren't so sure. Patti thought something else was wrong.

At eleven, Ramah was not ancient as black labs go, but she was certainly no spring chicken, and she had epilepsy. We had worried about her lack of mobility in Florida, but she had regained much energy in the move to a cool climate. Now, however, she was going downhill again.

"I'll have to take her to be looked at," Patti said, kneeling alongside her dog. Ramah had suffered epileptic seizures throughout her life and had never been spayed. Sometime during the winter, she had picked up an admirer, who sniffed around her scent and yellowed a few snowbanks. At first we thought it was a neighborhood dog, but we watched its tracks coming and going and realized it was probably a coyote. A dog would have come down the drive-

Sunset from our back deck.

way. This animal came out of the forest at times or left by way of the creek. Although we often looked out at the moon-lit snowdrifts at night, we had never seen either this proba-ble coyote or the fox that made a dainty, ruler-straight path down the driveway most nights.

That night, as the weather grew colder and the icicles at the eaves lengthened, we teased each other about our red-dened cheeks.

"You don't have to go to Florida to get a good tan," I said. "A couple of days like today would do the trick." Actually, our red faces were probably more a result of the wind than the sun, but the healthy color on our faces made us feel good. We had joked about going back to Florida and revealing our fish-belly white Minnesota skin for everyone to laugh at.

We also made a couple of phone calls to tease friends and relatives in the South, who, at the moment, had been encased in a cold wave. "Well, it was about fifty today up here and sunny enough for a sunburn. How about down there?"

As we enjoyed the glow of a great day, the temperature continued to fall, and winter returned. By morning, it was five above, and all that melted snow standing in puddles had turned to ice.

The Jeep, unknowingly positioned under a dripping eave overnight, had a ridge of ice across the top, and the driver's side door was frozen shut. "Back to reality," I said.

※ ※ ※

After the warm day, the snow developed a hard crust on top, strong enough to hold most small animals and even the larger, soft-padded ones like wolves, coyotes, and lynx. Only the moose and deer broke through, which tilted the odds in favor of predators that could travel fast across the top of the deep snow.

I don't remember being any other place that celebrated Valentine's Day as intensely as Grand Marais and vicinity. No doubt this had to do with the long winter and the fact that Valentine's Day fell smack in the middle of it, sort of like hump day mid-week.

The advertisements in the *Cook County News-Herald* beckoned. That night, Patti and I had dinner at Birch Terrace. For the first time in months, I was outdoors without wearing Sorel boots, and the restaurant's snow and ice-covered parking lot tilted toward the door. With my hard-soled shoes, I slid most of the way across the lot and ended up with the door in my hand.

We had a corner table overlooking the harbor, which surpisingly was free of ice due to the strong wind, and the sparkle of waves in the streetlights was a strange sight.

Although Lake Superior rarely froze to the horizon, we had grown accustomed to seeing a sheet of jagged ice on the harbor since Christmas.

We had a lovely candlelit dinner, with both of us feeling a bit strange in our dress-up clothes after six weeks in the woods in sweat suits, long underwear, and snowmobile gear.

Driving home on the snow-packed roads, it began to snow lightly. Our immediate, spontaneous response was, "Wonderful." We had not seen a good helping of fresh snow in about three weeks. We were ready for its cleansing beauty.

The snow didn't amount to much, perhaps an inch or so of fluff, and in the morning I swept it off the front walk and the back deck with the broom. As always, the four cats were in audience, lined up attentively along the sliding glass doors between living room and back deck.

As soon as I finished sweeping and Patti spread seeds along the seats and railing of the deck, the birds settled in for breakfast. Chickadees, nuthatches, jays, and grosbeaks were joined by a few purple finches, the vanguard of what would become a large contingent of little raspberry-colored birds. The cats also watched the birds, enthralled at their own live bird show, sometimes only inches from their hungry eyes. Tails swishing in anticipation, they occasionally even lunged at the glass, tempted beyond restraint by the feathered dinner just inches away.

Though they enjoyed the show, birds were not a part of their diets. They lived happily on a mixed blend of canned and dry cat food. When one of them caught and ate a deer mouse, it was always regurgitated.

Usually, the cats paired up for various activities.

Booter and Caesar hung out together, and Einstein and Sam made a second pair. Hearing a mouse in the wall, they'd pair up and wait all night if necessary for the mouse to come out. Mice are not all that smart, but our cats were well fed, and usually we'd save the mice before the cats got serious and killed them.

In the guest bedroom was an upper bunk reached by a ladder. Within a couple of months of our arrival, three of the cats learned to climb the ladder. It was warm up there, right next to the fireplace chimney, and they felt protected as well. Only Sammy, the three-legged cat, could not master the ladder.

Sam became the kitchen cat, jumping up on the stool to watch Patti prepare meals. At first, she would know his presence was a sign that the others had climbed the ladder, but by mid-winter, Sam spent time on the stool even when his buddy, Einstein, watched birds at the window or when all three of the others slept in a cat pile on our big bed upstairs.

For exercise and play, we'd tie a ball or some other item to a string, then roll it towards them and slowly twitch it back. Cats cannot resist this type of movement and will almost always jump at it. Sometimes, we could get them to chase the rolling ball or the rubber mouse on a long string for half an hour at a time. I'm sure they thought they were still kittens, because they still played together in that way.

Watching them chase and roll and bat the ball reminded me again of that afternoon the previous summer when we had seen the two cougar kittens playing just beyond the ditch as we drove by. We were startled by the sight—they were no bigger than our cats and engrossed in wrestling and tumbling with each other. As we passed by—it took my brain a few seconds to process the sight and stop the car. When we backed up, they were gone. No doubt mother was close by, and we certainly were not venturing into the woods to find out.

About that time, we had another cat episode. Looking out the dining room window, Patti saw something move up by our garden shed, which was about two hundred feet from the house.

"I think it was a fox," she said.

I questioned her. Was it orange? Yes. Was it the right size? Yes. Did it have a long, fluffy tail? Yes. Perhaps this was indeed the elusive night fox we'd never seen.

We started watching more closely, checking the shed from the window every hour or two. In a couple of days, Patti spotted it again. This time I brought the big field glasses.

"Is it the fox?" She asked excitedly.

"Not exactly," I replied.

"Well, then, what exactly is it?" She answered.

"Looks like a large, long-haired, orange-and-white cat."

"Let me look," she said, reaching for the glasses. "What's a cat doing up there?" She wondered, watching it disappear beneath the shed.

I shook my head. The cat had apparently found shelter there and had stayed awhile. We saw it once more, then it moved on. Despite our usual attempt at detective work, this became one more mystery that was never solved. The cat simply arrived one day, then a few days later it left. Who knows what the motivations were.

Looking out to see the "fox" up at the shed did alert us to another fact of which we'd been unaware. We discovered that Percy Partridge had become a more regular visitor than we knew. We watched him three times in two days as he flew to the cherry tree, chased away the tattletale blue jays, climbed stiffly into the feeding box we'd wedged in the head-high crotch where the branches met, and ate both bird seeds and sunflower seeds. Since the cherry tree was directly in front of the dining room window, we had a perfect view.

With six-inch wood sides, the box was just large enough for one partridge and provided at least a bit of protection. Percy would peck at the seeds awhile, then look around slowly for any lurking danger. He would spend maybe fifteen minutes in the box, then fly up to a large overhanging branch that grew from an adjacent spruce.

We concluded that Percy was a very brave bird, but also quite foolish for exposing himself to considerable danger. We had lost a suet slab just two nights earlier that had been hanging near the feeding box and decided it must be the work of our neighborhood marten.

12

❄ A Winter Vacation ❄

Mid-February and the Arrowhead of Northern Minnesota, as our region was called, was locked in a seemingly endless routine of cold and wind followed by more cold and light snow. For two mornings in succession, my writing suffered, became non-productive. The weatherman called these cycles "Alberta clippers," which seemed to me a too-cute way of describing bad weather.

After sitting more than an hour with ballpoint poised for an inspired thought to arrive, I pushed back the chair, went downstairs and arranged logs and kindling in the fireplace. Patti found me staring into the newly lit blaze.

"Okay, what's wrong?" She asked. "You never give up so early."

"I don't know. I just feel blah," I replied.

"As in blah sick or blah bored?" She asked.

I shrugged, then answered. "Can't seem to put anything on paper. Maybe it's what they call writer's block, but I think it's more like cabin fever."

"You want to get out of here for a while?"

I didn't know what I wanted. I guess it was a case of anticipations unfulfilled. I had thought we were going south but we weren't. I had expected the weather to be improving but it wasn't. "Let me think about it, okay?"

She nodded and petted the dog who had come over stiffly to sit at her feet. "We could go somewhere for a couple days. The cats will be fine here if we turn on electric heat, and Ramah can stay at the kennel in Duluth. I need provisions anyway."

I looked up. "That might be a good idea. Sure you don't mind?"

She shook her head and smiled. "Probably do us good."

"You game for Minneapolis? We could see the boys, go out for dinner, maybe even stop at Byerly's for some special groceries."

"Oh, could we?" She clapped her hands together and grinned. "I just love that store."

Patti had discovered Byerly's grocery store the previous summer and had never seen anything like it. She'd gladly make the four and one-half hour drive to see it again.

"If we're going, you better call Rob and Tom and make some dinner plans. I'll alert the neighbors so they can help keep an eye out. And let's not forget to ask Phil Hedstrom to stop by and check things."

I nodded, smiling as I watched her mind go into action. She hurried to her desk for a pad on which to make notes. Clearly she was as pleased with the idea of an excursion as I was.

By the time we set out the next morning, we had an itinerary, including dinner plans with the two sons that night, followed by a day of shopping. We loaded the Jeep, double checked the electric heat and set out into a blustery February day.

By the time we dropped Ramah and climbed the hill west of Duluth on I35, we found ourselves in a blizzard. Visibility dropped to about a hundred feet, and I slowed to shift into four-wheel drive.

"Thank God we've got an outfit that will take us through this," I said. "But if the visibility gets much worse, we'll have to pull off and stop."

We found we were able to drive about fifty miles per hour and feel somewhat safe. Still, whenever another car passed, it blinded us completely for several seconds. The best way to describe it is white-knuckle driving.

Part of it was the snow, but much of my fear came from the way other people were driving in what were very dangerous conditions. Some of them were flying by at least sixty-five miles per hour.

"That's totally insane," I said as a small econobox sailed past. "No wonder you hear of fifty-car collisions in fog or blowing snow. These people are flying blind. They can't possibly react to what's ahead because they can't see."

Just then, an eighteen wheeler came blazing by doing sixty, which so blinded me I had to slow to about twenty-five. At that moment, I had more fear of being hit from behind than of driving into the ditch.

We struggled on, at one point passing two cars in the classic T-bone position in the ditch. Finally, we reached a section of road protected by large spruce and pine from the wind and our visibility improved for a few miles. But only for a few miles. Then it was back to white out.

The weather improved slowly as we neared the Twin Cities, and we flowed with the rush-hour traffic around the north and west side of Minneapolis to our destination of Golden Valley.

Safely ensconced in our budget motel, I sat on the bed. It felt like someone was letting the air out of me.

"Tired?" Patti asked sympathetically, watching me deflate.

"I feel like I've run a marathon," I replied. Noting that we had an hour or so before it was time to leave for dinner, I laid back on the bed, closed my eyes and was instantly asleep.

That evening we met sons Rob, twenty-eight, and Tom, twenty-five, for dinner and conversation. Between the two we spent two and one-half hours at the table catching up on

their past few months. We also shared the adventures and
mis-adventures of our past winter up in the northwoods.

"You've only spent half the winter so far," Rob corrected.

I counted on my fingers. "We're in our fifth month. I hope
we're more than half way."

"Yes," he laughed, "but the best part is yet to come."

I rolled my eyes in mock horror. "You're talking about the
dreaded March blizzards?"

"And the April blizzards," he added.

"Maybe even a May blizzard," Tom pointed out.

"Okay, that's enough," Patti interrupted. "I'll never get
him back up there if you keep it up."

We talked and talked some more and made plans for
them to come up and visit us once fishing season was underway and winter was over.

"There will be snow on the ground in the woods, but I
think fishing opener officially qualifies as spring." I said.

"You hope," Tom said.

I nodded, remembering one year when I lived in subur-
ban Minneapolis and set out from there with a friend, Bill
Langsdorf, to open the fishing season on Saganaga at the
end of the Gunflint Trail. It was ninety when we left in shorts
and tee-shirts. By the time we reached Duluth, we'd lost
most of the fishing traffic, and it was cool enough to put on
long pants and sweatshirts. At Grand Marais, it was even
colder, so we donned jackets and stocking caps.

Finally, we reached Sag landing and met my dad. It was
nearly midnight and spitting snow. We loaded our gear, and
he ran us unerringly through the channels and around the
islands to the Canadian side and our rental cabin.

We awoke the next morning early with three inches of
snow covering the two boats. Although the ice was gone and
the water open, there was still some question whether it was
spring or still winter.

We said goodbye to the boys, and, in the morning, I
dropped Patti at Byerly's and went over to a couple of car

dealerships to look at vehicles I'd never seen on the road. Although Cook County had a Chevy-Olds dealer and Duluth had dealers for all the American brands and a couple of top Japanese labels, there were many cars that were not available anywhere between Grand Marais and Minneapolis. To see such cars as Mazda, Land Rover, and the German brands, I had to go to Minneapolis.

No, I wasn't planning to buy a new car. We were on a tight budget, but I'd seen a few 4X4s described in the auto magazines and wanted a closer look at what were considered off-brands or exotics on the north shore. I chuckled to myself, realizing that to Cook County drivers, our Jeep Cherokee must be considered exotic since the current body style was a year and a half old and yet ours was the only one in the county.

I picked Patti up as she was wheeling her cart down the final carpeted aisle at Byerly's. As we loaded food in the Jeep, we decided suddenly to head back home. One should take advantage of nice days, and this was one of them. The sun had melted much of the snow off the roads, and, since we'd accomplished our goals, we set off on the freeway for Duluth. As entertaining as it was to get away, we were even more eager to get back home. After living in the woods, the pace of the city felt uncomfortable. No discussion needed— we were ready and eager to go.

"So, did you see any nice cars?" Patti asked.

"Two or three, but without money, we can only look. Besides, the Cherokee has only got twenty thousand on it. Just getting broken in."

The highway was still wet and slushy in places but generally fast, and at 1:00 P.M. we parked in front of the Wholesale Food Club, where we bought things like soap and bleach for less. Even in Duluth, the streets were wet from a lovely winter day.

In twenty more minutes of driving, we were back on packed snow and arriving at the kennel, where Ramah was still stiff but joyful at our arrival. Her tail thumped against tables, chairs, and walls, as she limped along with us to the car.

Within twenty miles of Duluth, we saw our first deer. Packed along the Lake Superior shoreline as they were, it was impossible to drive Highway 61 without seeing them in large numbers. Clad in winter grey, they stood knee deep in the snow, casually watching as we passed. Were they safer from wolves when they stayed so close to the highway? I pondered the premise as our count increased to forty by Beaver Bay and seventy-five by Schroeder.

Twice we slowed to let deer cross ahead of us. Other times, the road would be covered with ravens feeding on the carcass of a not-so-fortunate casualty of the traffic. Near Tofte, a great huge eagle sat in a birch almost directly over the road, waiting to descend to a road kill. We slowed almost to a stop, but he only stared, unperturbed. And there we were without a camera.

Just beyond the rock cut, we saw the last two deer of our trip, making a total of one hundred eighteen, a sizeable count for one hundred miles, but far off the count of four hundred thirty-two that someone had told us about recently.

At five o'clock, when we reached Grand Marais and started up the long hill on the Gunflint Trail, it was still daylight, just sunset. The days were getting longer and I smiled. I had always grown a bit depressed at the lack of daylight in January, and now doctors had discovered the linkage between short days and troubled emotions. Just knowing the days were now a couple of hours longer made me feel better.

As we pulled into the driveway, Poe led us at eye level along its length, apparently eager to have Patti back after only a day and a half.

The house was warm and the cats lonesome when we got there. After unloading, I walked back to the corner of the driveway where something had made tracks.

"What is it?" Patti hollered from the driveway.

"Moose," I called back. "He's been wandering all over around here." Indeed, the big animal had been back and forth across the driveway a half dozen times.

I trudged through the snow up the hill toward the garden, following the trail of moose tracks until there was a deep hole in the snow that went all the way down to grass. The moose had dug at least three feet through hard-packed snow to get down there, but I wondered why. And then the answer hit me; that's where the salt lick was. Somehow he'd smelled the salt through all that snow.

I stood there, looking at the hole he'd dug, then scanned the darkening woods, but there were no unusual large dark shapes out there for now. Mister Moose had moved on.

❄ ❄ ❄

The next morning dawned overcast with a forecast of snow. We had gone through most of January and February with little snow, and what we had had settled a bit. But March was near, and with it would come the famous "state tournament" blizzards, along with more overall snow than any other month. The days may be getting longer, but the boys had been right; we weren't out of the woods, yet.

I was downtown filling up at Buck's when someone mentioned catching a nice mess of brook trout. Naturally, my ears perked up as snatches of conversation floated my way. "Big ones . . . road past Two Island . . . two days ago." I didn't know the men who were talking, so I waited until they paid and walked out the door before asking Buck if he'd heard them talking.

"They said something about going up past Two Island Lake and catching some big brookies," I explained.

He said he hadn't heard them, but the snatch of conversation got him thinking. "You know, if you go past Two Island and go west on the Grade, you're mostly into walleye lakes," he mused. "Wonder if they were talking about the Ballclub Road. There's a couple little trout lakes off to the west about halfway up the road, five miles or so."

"Oh, yeah," I replied, "we were in there last summer. Caught a couple of fifteen-inch trout one Sunday. Found a nice place to fish in there on the far side of the lake, past the island. I can't think of the name of it, but it will come to me."

"Bath Lake," Buck said with a smile and a finger raised to underscore his successful memory. "I'll bet that's what they were talking about."

"You think so?" I asked hopefully.

He nodded. "I know for a fact that three guys were in there a couple of weeks ago and did well." He said. "I can't think of anything else in that direction."

I thought for a moment about buying minnows and heading for Bath Lake but resisted the urge and went home baitless. I did, however, mention to Patti that I'd just overheard two men talking about catching brook trout there, and maybe we could think about taking a fishing trip soon.

For now, however, the snow was already falling and visibility was decreasing. There would be no fishing trip today. Instead, we watched as Bertha was joined by a chattering flock of small brown birds on the back deck.

We got out the bird books and started looking through them to identify our new visitors. They were the kind of featureless birds that I'd always lumped into the sub-category of "tweety bird" before, but now that we had at least thirty of them twittering and hopping along the railings, we had to have a better name.

Identifying a small brown bird using illustrations in a bird book is hopelessly confusing to a beginner. Once I stumbled into the sparrow pages, it got worse. Luckily, this bird was actually smaller than a sparrow, about the size of a wren. We finally settled on the siskin as a probable choice, but we were not certain until a couple of days later when we got the local *News-Herald* and read in Justine Kerfoot's column that the pine siskens had arrived at Gunflint Lake.

So now, in addition to our usual winter gang of birds, we had a growing flock of purple finches and a horde of pine siskens. Life was getting busier on the back deck and our cats, having stationed themselves along the glass sliders with twitching tails, were having the time of their lives watching the action.

13

❄ Brush with the Law ❄

I could not get Bath Lake out of my mind, and just thinking about the pretty little lake with the rocky island in the middle was too much temptation to withstand. So the next morning, after shoveling the four inches of snow off the deck and front walk, I drove downtown to pick up minnows and a Jerry can full of gas. Despite our ice fishing failures to date, the discouragement vanished when I thought about the trout awaiting us.

"Why do you think this will be different?" Patti asked.

"I can just feel it," I replied. "This will be good."

"Have you heard of guarded optimism?" She asked, trying to stifle a laugh.

"Of course. Absolutely. But why should I be guarded when I feel so sure of this. I really believe we're gonna catch fish," I declared.

"Okay, we'll go, but it's gonna snow some more. I can feel it," she said. Patti wasn't exactly negative but more or less concerned about what she thought was unwarranted optimism on my part.

"You're right, we might not catch a thing, but the outing will be good for us, get us out for some exercise." I said.

So, at my urging, we set out for Two Island Lake and the Ballclub Road, which was not plowed. We parked and unloaded the snowmobile, then set out to travel five miles north on the packed trail.

It was snowing steadily, hard wind-blown pellets from the northeast, when we turned up the narrow cut through the woods that was the old tote road leading to Bath Lake. The snow was unbroken, as though nobody had gone there.

"Well, that's either good news or bad news," I said, shrugging. Nobody had been in there for a while, I was certain.

I gunned Orange Julius, and we climbed the steep grade from the Ballclub Road into the woods, then settled down to a steady pace. Two miles later, we were stopped at the edge of Bath Lake, looking out into the snow at the indistinct outline of the island.

"I'll cut across the bay and follow the shoreline on the left," I said, turning back to Patti. She nodded and we hummed out across the lake, setting off clouds of blowing snow in our wake. We ran along the east shore and stopped where the island and shoreline were only fifty yards apart.

"This looks good," I said, pulling to a stop and dismounting. I stood back to the wind and snow and cleared a small area of the snow that lay deep on the ice. Patti helped, and we enlarged the bare area until I could stand on the ice and start to turn the hand auger.

When the ice is only twelve to fourteen inches thick, a manually turned ice auger works well, but later in the winter, when the ice can reach a thickness of thirty inches or more, drilling a hole can be a killing task. Then the man with a gas powered auger is king.

There was no gas auger here, just the two of us breathing heavily and staring at a hole no deeper than a few inches. I leaned on the auger another half minute, then started drilling again. Another two or three inches. Patti tried and got perhaps an inch. Then my turn again.

"I think this is what causes people to have heart attacks," I said between breaths. Both our faces were red from the cold and the exertion, and I was feeling shaky.

We worked slowly for as long as we could, then rested again. The hole was another two inches deep. Fifteen minutes of work and sixteen inches of hole. I was beginning to wonder if we'd ever get to fish.

The hole took twenty-five minutes to drill and left us both shaking with exhaustion. Then we sat on the snowmobile for five minutes more to catch our breaths.

"I think we'll start with just one," I said, trying to laugh. Patti agreed with a nod. We had yet to learn that she was suffering from high blood pressure and that work like this could be dangerous.

After baiting up a hand line and letting it down near the bottom, we sat together on the snowmobile seat, resting and catching our breaths. The line rested quietly, tempting nothing down below.

And then we heard the far-off sound drift down on the wind. I listened. Chainsaw? Snowmobile? It was hard to tell. It faded for a few seconds, then came back, faintly at first, then louder. A snowmobile. This time I was certain.

"You hear it?" I said.

"Yes," she replied. "Snowmobile?"

I nodded, then got up to listen. The machine was traveling fast along the north shore of the lake. Would it pass us by or follow our trail out onto the ice?

The sound preceded its coming, and we could hear it growing louder as it came toward us on the lake before we could make out its vague dark outline in the falling snow.

I would be less than candid if I said I was not more than a little bit apprehensive at its approach. Why would anybody be running so hard in our wake, traveling seven miles or more from where we parked to track us down?

The big machine pulled up within a few feet of us, and its driver stood up and dismounted quickly, removing his helmet.

"Hi, I'm Dale Horner, the game warden," he said. "May I see your fishing licenses?"

The tension broke, and I smiled. "Give me a minute to dig 'em out." I unzipped my snowmobile suit and dug in my pocket clumsily to get the pack of cards and licenses.

"Okay," I said, shuffling the cards. "Here are the licenses." I handed him the two licenses I'd purchased when we arrived. They were out-of-state licenses, and I explained that we'd just moved here and become residents.

"How many holes have you drilled?" He asked. I showed him the only hole and was about to make a joke when he changed the subject.

"How many fish have you got?" He asked.

"None," I said, "we're just getting started."

He nodded, glanced again at the license and handed them back to me.

"Looks okay," he said. "Have a good day of fishing."

"Thanks," I replied.

He turned, picked up his helmet, climbed aboard his snowmobile and started it with a button. Then he looped around us and pulled away, back in the direction he'd come, leaving us standing in the snow.

"Well, that was something," I said.

"Did he come all this way just to check our licenses?" Patti asked.

"I guess so," I answered, looking down at the pieces of colored paper that were open in my hand. I raised them and took a better look, then said to myself, "Oh, my God."

"What is it?" Patti asked.

"These licenses run out the last day of February," I said. "That's today. We're lucky this wasn't tomorrow, or we'd be paying some serious fines."

I shook my head, surprised he hadn't mentioned that fact, a bit surprised at the entire episode.

"Well, let's get back to fishing," I said. "I'll start working on another hole out further."

Twenty minutes later, we had a second hole drilled fifty feet closer to the island. After a few minutes of rest, I set up the rig with a stick to warn us if a fish grabbed the minnow.

And then we began the long wait that every ice fisherman experiences, sitting quietly watching our lines and from time to time getting up to clean skim ice from the holes. In this case, we were also getting covered by the falling snow.

"This is why I hate ice fishing," Patti said. "It's bor-ing! At least with regular fishing I can cast, do something, even if the fish don't bite."

"Well, this wouldn't be boring if we caught fish," I replied, for the sake of argument.

"But we don't catch fish, so it's boring."

I nodded my snow-covered head, chagrined by the circumstances that led to us being here.

"You're right," I said. "This is ridiculous. We need to take up something more active." A thought sailed by. "How'd you like to learn cross-country skiing? That way we'd be outdoors, but we'd be getting some exercise."

"I could do that," Patti said. "I'd much rather do that than this."

"Okay, let's try it. I can rent us some skis down at Joynes' store so we can see if we like it."

Patti nodded solemnly in agreement, then spread her arms beseechingly, "Does that mean we can end this and go home?"

I laughed out loud. "Sure, I guess so. This isn't doing us any good. You were a good sport to go along on what turned out to be another wild-goose chase."

Ten minutes later, we had loaded our gear and tied it down with bungee cords. Old reliable growled to life on the second pull, and we set off into the heavily falling snow.

The game warden's trail was almost obscured by new snow as we crossed the lake and rode into the woods. It occurred to me that we were seven miles from the car and probably fifteen miles from the nearest occupied house in the middle of a snowstorm. I looked back out across the lake; where there had been an island was now only a blur of falling snow. Visibility was about a block.

The wind blew from the east, which meant that at least a part of this snow was due to lake effect. Warm, moist lake air blowing across the cold snow-covered hills. It's the reason Michigan's Upper Peninsula gets two hundred fifty inches of snow each winter. And now we were the target.

With the deep new snow and limited visibility, we ran at about fifteen miles per hour back to the Ballclub Road and down to the car, which was now only a car-like shape beneath a seven- or eight-inch mantle of white. It was amazing how much snow had fallen so quickly. And now I had to drive in it.

With four-wheel drive, the deep snow was not a problem. But the visibility was bad because the snow stuck and had to be removed by windshield wipers that iced up. Twice we stopped to clear the wipers and check the trailer. The snow was so deep in places that the belly of the Jeep dragged. There was no traffic on the back road between Two Island Lake and Devil's Track; in winter it was kept open primarily for logging since nobody lived in the area.

Taking it slow, we finally arrived at the north side of Devil's Track Lake—civilization. A few people lived along the lake year-round, so the road was usually well-maintained. But on this day, we could hardly recognize the intersection, much less see the lake.

We turned east and kept moving, slower now because we were going into the wind and the visibility was even worse. I was reminded of a South Dakota blizzard I experienced as a teenager. Visibility was so bad I had to get out and walk ahead through the drifting snow. Dad had put the chains on the back tires to give us traction.

I started telling the story to Patti, and her first question was, "Do you want me to get out and walk ahead? Is that what you're saying?"

"No, no, of course not. We're doing just fine," I said quickly.

She sat eyeing me with skepticism.

"If anybody's gonna get out and walk ahead, it will be me." I added. "But it's not necessary. I was just telling a story. That's all."

Actually, we were rolling along at fifteen miles an hour and now, in the lee of the trees, we could see somewhat better.

At the Gunflint Trail, our prospects improved because the plows had made a pass each way and cut away a lot of snow. We drove up the trail to our driveway, where we plowed through a two-foot-deep windrow and sort of floated along on the deep snow to the garage.

"I think we're home for the night," I said. "At least the electricity works, and we've got plenty to eat."

Later that night, the snow stopped falling. In the morning, while shoveling, we estimated the new snow at about fifteen inches. It was the first of March, and we had a lot of winter to go.

14

❄ The Energizer Bunny ❄

We received no new snow for several days, and, true to my word, I rented two pairs of cross-country skis. The big day was pleasant and sunny, about twenty degrees, and, after a few short practice runs on the driveway, we drove a mile north to George Washington State Forest, where a two mile loop trail ran among the red pines. As ski trails go, it was somewhat shorter and flatter than most, which suited us to a "T."

There were two cars in the lot, and one group still there getting ready to go when we pulled in. I got the skis and poles out and placed them next to the Jeep so we could step in and clamp them while leaning on the car for support.

After struggling a couple of minutes, we were both in our skis and ready for action. The other group seemed to be standing around talking.

"Ready to go?" I asked.

"Let's wait a minute," Patti said.

"Why? What's wrong? You okay?"

"Yes, I'm okay," she said in a low voice. "I just want to wait for that other bunch to go first."

I shrugged and nodded okay, and we waited thirty seconds. The other group seemed intent on talking.

"We can't wait forever," I said. "Let's roll."

Patti still looked perplexed and unsure, so I waved her along toward the trail.

"C'mon on," I said with a reassuring smile. "Nothing bad can happen."

Famous last words. The trail started with a little one-foot dip. It couldn't have been more than that, but it was enough to send my skis forward while my body was still leaning back. Whoof, I landed on my back in the deep snow. All was silent. No doubt I was the center of attention.

I floundered about in the snow for a minute or so, knowing everyone was watching and probably rolling their eyes at each other. It should have been easy to get back up, but it wasn't. Finally, I climbed hand over hand up one of the ski poles and stood up, knocking snow of my clothes.

I glanced at the people standing no more than twenty feet away, watching me.

"Just learning," I said with an attempt at a chuckle. They nodded, smiling now. Any idiot could see I was a novice, wearing wool pants and a snowmobile jacket. They certainly didn't need to be told.

"You okay?" Patti asked, trying hard to look solemn.

"Oh, sure, just entertaining the crowd," I said. "You ready to go?"

This time, the little hill didn't trip me up, and I skied off in what felt like perfect form, with Patti following closely.

"You want to lead?" I asked.

"No, I'm happy this way," she replied.

I skied away again. She was still on my heels. So I skied faster. Still she hung close. I stopped again.

"Why don't you lead? Maybe you ski faster than I do."

"Well, you're going slow. Maybe you could go just a little bit faster."

"I am going faster. Here, go on by." I stepped aside and let her go past on the track. Within five minutes, she was well ahead, and I was hurrying to keep her in sight. No matter how I tried, I couldn't keep up, let alone catch her.

We stopped at a trail junction where the snow was riddled with moose tracks. Somehow, feeling clumsy on my skiis, the sight of all those moose tracks gave me pause. There was no way I could get out of the way if one of those furry locomotives came trotting down the path. Luckily, the moose were somewhere else right then, no doubt plotting strategy.

"Well, you were certainly moving along," I said. "You're doing well."

She smiled. "It's fun, and I feel comfortable out here."

"I'm working on my style," I said. "I'll pick up the speed later." I was not about to tell her I couldn't keep up. No sir. Just because my wife could ski like the Energizer Bunny didn't force me to admit defeat. Not yet anyway. How could this be happening?

The cross-country ski trail near our house.

Then I thought of another excuse. "Besides, how can you race through this beautiful forest?" Indeed, the scene was simply magnificent, with shafts of sunlight cutting through the tall canopy of red pines to highlight a world of sparkling white velvet.

The pines had been planted during World War II by the local Boy Scout troop and were now sixteen to twenty inches in diameter and seventy-five feet tall. The popular cross country trail meandered through their shadows from the Gunflint Trail to Elbow Creek and then along its banks before looping back.

Overhead, a gust of wind moaned through the upper branches, prompting them to dance in harmony and discharge clumps of snow that shattered on the lower branches and covered us with a cascade of sparkling snow dust.

Patti looked up and smiled, captured by the magic of the moment.

"Isn't this wonderful," she exclaimed, pulling on her gloves and gripping the poles. "If I seem to be hurrying, it's because I want to see what's up ahead." With that comment, she moved swiftly away. It was catch-up time once more as she rounded a curve along the river bank and disappeared from sight.

Though I set out in hot pursuit, I did not catch her until she stopped on a small hill to wait for me. Her speed was effortless and her breathing normal, while I gasped for air.

"The Energizer Bunny," I said after several deep breaths. "That's what you are. I think we've finally discovered your sport."

She grinned and nodded. "I really like this, and it's not all that hard."

I laughed. "You mean you want to be a granola-eating, skinny skier? First cousin to a tree hugger?"

She looked at me seriously, "I'm not a tree hugger."

"I know, but that's the stereotype that's spread by snowmobliers."

She shrugged. It didn't matter. Cross country skiing was fun, good exercise, and quiet. And we both agreed it beat ice fishing.

※ ※ ※

We kept the skis an extra day to do another loop of George Washington Forest. Before we went out to the car to make the short drive up the Gunflint, I envisioned all those moose tracks we'd seen the last time.

"Ya know what I'll bet?" I said.

"What?" She replied.

"I'll bet we see a moose today."

"Don't say that," she scowled. "Whenever you've said that, we have seen nothing. It's like your own personal hex. You predict a moose; there's no moose. You predict fish, no fish. I'd love to see a moose, but there's no chance to see one now. We might as well stay home."

I knew she was kidding me, sort of, but there was a grain of truth in what she said. I was always predicting this and that, but of late, my batting average was pretty low. Maybe I should rein in my urge to be the great know-it-all.

"All right, guilty as charged," I confessed. "No more predictions. We see what we see. Whatever happens, happens."

"That sounds good to me," Patti answered, hiding a little smile behind her hand.

We made the loop at George Washington and saw zero moose, as expected. And of course, also as expected, it was all my fault. Once again, the Energizer Bunny ran off and left me gasping for breath. Just another day on the cross-country trail. But, always the optimist, I was certain my skiing would improve amazingly as I rounded into shape.

※ ※ ※

Temperatures in the high thirties and warm sunshine curbed our skinny skiing and started a cycle that would last for nearly six weeks. During the day, melting occurred, turning snow and ice to water. And then at night when temperatures fell, water became ice again.

The first effect of this cycle was a dripping leak in the ceiling of my office. Since the ceiling consisted of tongue in groove boards, there was no way of knowing the exact location or source of the leak.

I went out the office window and stood on the snow-covered lower level roof to see if I could discover the reason for this drip. The cause was both obvious and ominous. In the course of the winter, a huge ice ramp or ice dam had built up on the edge of the roof. At the eaves, it was easily a foot thick. Unable to get past this ice dam, the runoff water backed up into the house.

Only one solution: get on the upper roof, above the ice, and chop channels through it with an axe so the melt water could run off. My love of high places, together with the effort required to chop through ice, put this job right up there with ice auguring as "most likely to cause a heart attack."

Patti, as always, was eager to help, but I said no, not this time. This was not like splitting firewood, where one good blow often did the job. The ice came off in maddeningly small chips, so I had to keep chopping. Patti and Bertha stood below offering encouragement, while Poe circled overhead cawing, but nothing made the work easier.

That day, I cut four channels in the ice and chopped holes in two shingles. They'd have to be replaced come summer. But the water quit leaking through the roof. The next morning, I added two more channels. Now we would have to wait and see.

As it turned out, the wait would be short. I no sooner came off the roof that the flakes began to fly. It was in the twenties so the snow was wet, heavy and thick.

15

❄ Stuck and Stuck Again ❄

Patti had been invited to lunch in town. By the end of the winter, she had become a good snow driver, so, even though it was snowing, she went ahead with her plans to do some errands and have lunch with two of my aunts and a cousin. I knew it would do her good to get out and see people.

"You think it'll be okay?" She asked, looking out at the snow.

I shrugged. "Sure. This snow could be over in a half hour. Just take it easy and call if there's a problem. You'll be fine."

She backed the Jeep out and disappeared in the murk while I went up to write for my allotted three or four hours. I was in a critical part of the book where I didn't really know how to make things come out, so I was intent on my work and not paying much attention to the weather outside.

I looked out to ponder something or another and suddenly realized I was looking at snow but nothing else. The big pines just past the garden were blotted out. It was really coming down. Still, she must be downtown. It could be much lighter there. So I refocused on the book and kept working.

At noon I looked out again to see the same scene as before. This time I got up and went downstairs to fix a bowl of soup for lunch. I also called Aunt Mae and asked to speak to Patti.

"It's snowing pretty hard up here, so be sure you're in four-wheel drive before you leave town," I said.

"Okay, we're going to eat, then I'll pick up a few groceries and come home. It's not snowing too bad in town," she replied.

"Have fun and don't come rushing home. Things will be fine. See you soon."

As I ate, the snow fell even harder. It's hard to imagine the intensity of lake-effect snow. The depth on the deck railing already measured six or seven inches.

I went downstairs where I was building more shelves for canned goods. It was a cool area where things would store well. After putting the last two one- by-twelve boards in place, I went back upstairs and out into the garage to put away nails and tools. I hadn't really looked at the weather since about twelve thirty or so, more than an hour earlier.

On the back deck, the snow depth was at least twelve inches. I didn't think it was possible for snow to accumulate that fast. I worried briefly, then shrugged. The Jeep would get her home even in a foot of new snow. No need to worry.

At two thirty I called Aunt Mae again. Patti had been gone about an hour. Mae guessed there were three or four inches of snow, "not too bad" as she put it. I said there was a lot more up here, but things would probably be fine.

I waited some more, then put on my "shoveling" clothes and went out back to clear the deck. By the time I finished, twenty minutes later, there was already an inch of fresh snow where I'd started.

It was after three by then and still no sign of her, just the snow falling heavily. Visibility must be terrible. I imagined all kinds of scenarios.

At three-thirty, I heard the garage door roll up. Immediate relief flooded over me. All was well. I looked out. No car. Then Patti opened the door between the walkway and house. She was covered with white and out of breath, carrying a snow-covered bag of groceries.

Before I could ask what happened, she blurted out the bad news. "Car's stuck—right by the mailbox. Up on a pile of snow. The wheels just spin." She stopped to take a couple of deep breaths. "Had to walk up the driveway. The snow is really deep."

"Hey, as long as you're okay, that's all that matters," I said, taking the groceries. "You get your heavy stuff off, and I'll go shovel out the car."

"You won't believe it," she said, still breathing heavily. "Snow's up to here," she added, pointing to her knees.

I shook my head. "How was it coming up the hill?" I asked.

"That wasn't bad. At least the plow had been through. It was just where we pull in that it was too deep, even for the Jeep."

We talked briefly, and I started back down the driveway with shovel in hand. It was deep, all right, about a foot and a half. This would be hard going for the Jeep even if I got it shoveled out.

When I got to the car, I could see it was high centered on the ridge thrown up by the plow. No way for the four-wheel drive to grip. So after a couple of minutes to catch my breath, I started moving snow.

It took fifteen minutes per side to clear the snow from beneath the sides, and I had no idea if that would be enough, since there was still snow in the middle packed underneath. But I tried it anyway. The wheels gripped, then spun.

More shoveling underneath. I could actually feel the car settle. Another try. The Jeep moved a foot then spun, so I backed it up two feet, rocked it forward about five feet, then backed out onto the road where the snow was only a few inches deep.

With poor visibility, it was dangerous to leave the car crosswise on the Gunflint Trail, so I pulled forward and started uphill on the driveway. Thirty feet later, pushing a huge mound of snow, it spun and stopped.

Back down the driveway for another try. This time I got to the crest of the hill. Daylight was failing, so I turned on the lights and went again. This time, going slightly downhill, the Jeep burrowed forward a couple of hundred feet.

I kept backing and running forward several more times before nearly reaching the dry garage. It was five thirty, and the snow was still falling. One more run at it down the hill should do it, I thought.

This time, though, the Jeep slid to the left down into a depression, with the driver's side against the six-foot snowbank created by plowing. The car wouldn't budge, and I had to climb over to the passenger side to get out.

Admitting defeat, I slogged the short distance to the garage, stomped off the snow and went inside. We'd have to wait for Greg to plow before the Jeep could be extracted. Where he was going to put all this snow was anybody's guess.

Inside, it was a great night for hot soup and a crackling fire in the big stone fireplace. Patti had the soup ready, and I lit the birch and kindling as we settled in to spend a cozy night at home.

❉ ❉ ❉

In the morning, the snow was replaced by the kind of cold, bright day that belonged in January. As it was a Saturday, Greg arrived in mid-morning to plow. I went out to greet him.

"Slid down on that ice," he said, looking at the Jeep. "Shouldn't be hard to get it out, once I clear some of the driveway."

"You got room for all this snow?" I asked.

"No," he grinned. "Not really. I'll have to get the skip loader and push it back again. Not much we can do about that. If this was the end of March, I'd say let's try to get by.

But we've got a lot more of March left, so we might get quite a bit more snow."

I nodded, accepting his judgement.

After he made a few runs with the plow, we hooked a chain to the trailer hitch of the Jeep, and I crawled inside and started her up. Once free of the snowbank, it was easy to back out, then pull ahead into the garage.

Greg managed to clear the parking turn-around area enough to be useable, then did the driveway just about the width of his blade before he left with the promise of returning in a couple of days with the big loader.

We celebrated with a walk to the mailbox wearing dark glasses to cut the white glare of fresh snow. My eyes in particular had lost their ability to adapt to darker interiors after being out in the sun without sun glasses, so I wore them regularly outdoors.

As we set out, the strangest call echoed through the woods. I'd heard it before but had never identified the bird that made it. It was a large bird, and if it had been summer, I'd have guessed it was a heron or marsh bird of some kind. It started low, then warbled into a high note, then back down low. Probably the strangest bird call I'd ever heard.

"Did you hear that?" I said, stopping in my tracks.

Patti nodded. We stood still to see if it was repeated, and in a few seconds it was, the same discordant yet melodic series of low and high notes.

My eyes went to the source of the song and there, atop the garden shed, sat a lone raven. He arose and flapped over us, talking in his usual gutteral voice.

"I've heard that song before, but I never knew it came from a raven," I said, really amazed at the bird's ability to change voices.

The big bird flew ahead, then sat on a limb awaiting us as we walked. I suppose he expected Patti to lay a few morsels on the snowbank as we passed beneath his perch. When we kept going, he simply flew ahead and waited again.

As we crested the last rise before the driveway fell away to the main road, Patti spotted a movement.

"There, in the hazelbrush," she said, pointing.

Sitting perfectly still, the snowshoe hare probably thought he was invisible. But there was a second hare in the thick brush, and his movement had given them both away.

Although we had seen a virtual maze of tracks in the snow in and around the underbrush thicket, we had seen no rabbits for nearly five months. The last one we'd seen had been part brown, part white, in the middle of his fall color change. These two were both pure white, and sitting still behind the bushes, they were next to impossible to pick out. They were the first we'd spotted during daylight hours.

We stood for a couple of minutes watching. Then both of the hares hopped further into the thick brush and vanished. They were probably still watching us, invisible to our eyes, as we passed by on our way to the mailbox.

There was just enough room on our plowed driveway for one car to pass. It was easy to understand Greg's concern that another heavy snowfall would make it impossible to plow.

Poe accompanied us all the way to the road and back to the house, where Patti did, indeed, snatch a few leftovers to put out for him. It was a cold morning, but a beautiful one, and the walk proved that adventure and excitement could be and often was just around the corner if we were willing to get out and look for it.

※ ※ ※

The weather warmed, and the cycle of thaw and freeze returned. It was nearly time for the state high school basketball tournament, traditionally a weekend of snowstorms and blizzards, with thousands of people marooned and unable to travel. The weatherman ominously predicted a severe weather disturbance but was unable to pin down the exact path this possible storm would take.

The tournament started, and the weather turned bad, windy and overcast and threatening snow. Almost in unison, people around town warned that "this would be the big one." Greg finished pushing back the snowbanks along our driveway, and Patti and I felt relieved. Everybody's breath was held. It was already snowing in the Dakotas and western Minnesota, the blizzard warnings were officially posted, and then Mother nature changed her mind as the snow slid to the north and missed us by no more than a hundred miles.

"For once, I'm not disappointed," I said. "We've got three or four feet of snow on the level, and that's enough to last for a long while. Plus, there's no doubt we'll get some extra new snow to keep everything all white and wintry looking 'til May."

"'Til May?" Patti asked. "Are you sure?"

"Maybe just 'til early May," I laughed, "but there will still be some of it left in the woods on fishing opener. That's the middle of May, but it's almost a sure thing. You can count on having snow in the woods on opening weekend."

* * *

The sun was stronger now and had more bite against the south facing snowdrifts and the hard-packed snow on the back roads. Driving in slush became commonplace, and it was advisable to fill our windshield washer bottle.

I discovered this first-hand while following a pulp-wood truck down the Gunflint Trail one day on my way to see Virgil Lindquist, our insurance agent.

Virgil announced that we should get all questions answered right away because he was going to Mexico on his annual Easter vacation. When I suggested it was a little late for a winter vacation, what with spring coming on and all, he laughed and said most everybody he knew would be taking off in April. "It's traditional around here," he said. "When we get back in late April, we will have missed all that nasty stuff. We can start thinking about opening the cabin up for the summer."

Since Virgil was a lifelong resident and an old hand at such things, I had no choice but to believe him. It surprised me, but after thinking about it, I could certainly agree. It was sort of a reward one bestowed on oneself for having stuck it out through the winter.

But that day and the next two days in succession, the sun worked its magic. After three warm, bright days, the back deck was clear of snow and meltwater. The driveway was softening, and there was a small snowless spot up near the garden. In the war of seasons, spring was making its presence felt.

Easter Sunday dawned warm and sunny, with a pileated woodpecker hammering on a nearby tree. Patti went out to feed the birds, and a chickadee landed on her shoulder, as if to say, "Hi. I know you."

We drove down to Bethlehem Lutheran Church early to get our usual seats for the service, and instead of parkas and snowpants and fur hats, people were actually dressed in suits and pastel dresses. Some of the elderly ladies even sported Easter bonnets. It was a glorious day, with parts of the lawn starting to peek through the snow.

The minister gave an Easter message of renewal and rebirth and said that although we had no apple blossoms as did our capitol of Washington, D.C., there were reports coming in of pussy willows and crocuses, our first two signs of new life.

Arriving home, we heard the wild and inspiring cackle of geese and looked up to see a V of honkers overhead, flying north. Where in the world would they be heading? Didn't they know that everything was frozen over?

As we discovered that very afternoon, they knew things that we didn't. The snow was too sticky for skiing, so we got in the car and took a long drive on the South Brule Road and then the Lima Mountain Road, both of which had been plowed because logging was underway in those areas.

The Lima Mountain Road runs upstream along Fiddle Creek for a couple of miles until it reaches the headwater, part of which is a large, shallow pond about five acres in size. The creek was partly open and running, the water black against the sparkling snow. Nothing could be called unexpected until we rounded the bend and caught our breath at the sight; an open pond filled with thousands of geese. The sight was incredible, and the geese simply watched us as we drove by instead of panicking and flying away.

No sooner had we passed the pond than we met a pickup truck with a plow coming the other way. I pulled over slightly to pass and discovered that what I'd pulled out onto was not road but loose snow. We slid down into the ditch, and there we hung at a forty-five degree angle.

Fortunately, the pickup stopped and backed up. A solid man with a wind-burned face got out wearing his Carhart work jacket. He introduced himself as John Henry Eliason, who was logging near Lima Mountain.

He immediately offered assistance so we hooked the trailer hitch with a length of chain, and he easily pulled us up and out. He told us we'd have to turn around up ahead and come out since the road past the Lima Mountain turnoff wasn't plowed.

We thanked him and I drove on, mentally berating myself for getting stuck twice in less than three weeks with a four by four. Rumors to the contrary, no vehicle is immune from getting stuck. With a four by four, it was possible to get stuck worse when it happens.

We turned around and came back, with the road becoming more slushy from the sun's heat. In some places, our tires went through the slush to the mud below. The driving was getting worse, and I took it more slowly knowing how easily we could slide off the narrow road yet again. Now, that would be embarrassing.

16

✳ Death and Strange Behavior ✳

When we got back home it was sunny and warm but there was no dog at the door to meet us. Ramah had been virtually unable to stand that morning; her back legs kept giving out, and we knew the end was near. Now Patti hurried in and found her paralyzed from the waist down, unable to even make an attempt to stand. We tried to encourage her but there was nothing we could do.

In the morning, I carried Ramah to the Jeep and Patti drove to the vet's office, where the vet came out and looked her over before agreeing there was nothing that could be done for a dog of her age and condition.

The vet put her to sleep, and Patti cried all the way home at the loss of her longtime friend.

When she got home, we put Ramah in a large foot locker with her favorite blanket. I had already spotted a small, south facing rise beyond the garden where the sun had melted the snow away, leaving bare grass and dirt.

It took until late afternoon to dig down through the shale and rocks about four and one-half feet, and then we put the locker in the ground and said our tearful prayers of farewell for the old lab.

I marked the grave with a small cairn of rocks which was visible from the house. Two days later, after digging a channel that allowed the meltwater to cross the driveway on its path down to the creek, I looked up at the cairn and decided to walk up there to put a few more rocks on the mound.

After putting a couple of dozen more rocks on the pile, I noticed that the snow had retreated across the south-facing hill nearly to the garden. Even though it was still cold, the sun's power was doing its work.

I looked over at the shed, then stopped. At the base of the shed, a coyote lay curled up in the sun's rays. At first, I thought it was sleeping. I was hesitant about approaching it. Then, seeing it wasn't moving, I rolled a rock over against it. Again no movement. The coyote was dead, no more than fifteen feet from Ramah's grave.

The animal had definitely not been there two days earlier, of that I was certain. But somehow, this old coyote had chosen this very spot to curl up and die. Coincidence? Not likely.

Somehow, this coyote must have been Ramah's secret admirer all this time, visiting often to add his scent to hers. Then, old or sick, he had followed her scent to the grave and curled up close by, where he had died naturally.

Without touching him, I got Patti and had her come up to see for herself. She agreed with my theory, even though it might seem oddly coincidental. There really was no other explanation.

I dug a small hole near Ramah's grave for the old coyote and placed him there. When I picked him up, his body was surprisingly light, and I feel sure that sick or old, he had starved to death.

That night, I went to a regular committee meeting at the Lutheran Church. While I was waiting with two others for enough members to make a quorum, I told the strange sad story of our old lab and the coyote. They agreed it was something they'd never heard of or experienced before.

Ultimately, we gave up and went home because there was no quorum. Five of the twelve members were gone on vacation. Virgil Lindquist was right.

The next morning dawned overcast, and I went back to the garden shed to check that the graves hadn't been disturbed. It was a needless trip, but it allowed me to see a strange ritual going on nearby in our woods.

What caught my eye was the pileated woodpeckers hopping along stiff-legged on the crusted snow surface. I'd never seen one on the ground before. The big woodpecker was followed by a second woodpecker hopping along on his trail. They looked like prehistoric birds on pogo sticks.

The first bird jumped up on the trunk of a tree, then climbed and circled it about ten or fifteen feet. The second bird followed. Then the leader went back down the trunk and crossed the snow to climb another trunk.

Both birds were close to me but seemed to pay me no attention. I decided that Patti needed to see this strange business, so I moved cautiously away, ran down to the house and called her to put on a coat and boots and to hurry along and see something.

Out of breath and excited, I tried to fill her in on what was happening as we trotted along the driveway, then walked across the crusted snow. But of course, it would be better to see

Though they are difficult to see, two pileated woodpeckers sit low on tree trunks.

for herself if the woodpeckers were still busy with what I thought was some kind of courtship ritual.

Fortunately, they were still at it, climbing, circling and crossing to another tree. I whispered to Patti what I thought was going on, but she pointed out that both of the birds looked like males.

We watched for a half an hour, at which time Patti said she had washing to put in the dryer and left me alone with the birds, who kept up their display. I spent another half an hour, then went back to start on my own tasks, convinced that the birds planned to keep hopping and climbing, one after another, until they got bored with it or dropped from exhaustion.

Since we couldn't figure out what was going on with these woodpeckers, we called the local bird expert, who advised us that it was a territorial pre-mating thing that males did. He said we were fortunate to see it because it was an unusual thing for such shy birds to allow people to watch.

While standing in the woods, I'd heard a partridge drumming off to the north. It was the first I'd heard and I mentioned it to Patti.

"Wonder if it was Percy," she said.

I shook my head. "I don't know, it seems a bit early for them to start drumming to find a mate."

We talked about it and agreed that the next time we heard one, we'd go and try to find him. If we got close enough to see the bird, we could get a good photo for our animal album.

Sure enough, the very next day we heard one faintly drumming to the east, perhaps close to the driveway where it opened to the Gunflint. We got the camera with the long lens and started down the drive. At the corner, we heard the partridge drum again. This time, it was more noticeable that the drumming had a muffled quality instead of its usual resonance.

It came from up ahead, just around the curve in the drive, so we went cautiously along, looking for a log on which the partridge might be perched. During mating season, these partridges, officially known as ruffed grouse, stand on hollow logs or other downed trees and dead falls so that, when they beat their wings to call a mate, the flapping creates a resonant, drumming sound that is often quite loud.

Patti stopped and touched my arm. "On the right side of the driveway, sitting on the snow bank. Isn't that a partridge?" She whispered.

At first I didn't see the big bird against the brown background of brush and tree limbs. Then he moved, and his outline became clear.

"Stop here," I muttered. "Let's see what he does."

What we had both noticed was that Percy, as we always called him, was not standing on a log or a fallen tree but on a snow bank. He made no effort to find a log before he started drumming again.

I grinned at the bird on the snow bank. No wonder the sound doesn't carry, I thought. It probably couldn't be heard more than a hundred yards, which was about how far he was when we heard him faintly from near the garage.

After listening to a couple of feeble sounds, I touched Patti's arm, and we turned back. Halfway to the car, I rolled my eyes and snorted. "If that's Percy, he is one dumb bird," I said. "He's supposed to be on a log that causes the sound to echo, not on a snow bank," I added. "He'll exhaust himself without ever accomplishing a darn thing."

From time to time, we'd hear Percy's faint drumming and shake our heads. It wasn't until a month later when his favorite snow bank had melted that he found an old log and achieved some serious volume in his calls. Then he became a boomer, as partridges are sometimes called.

❋ ❋ ❋

In the early morning, after a cold night had hardened the surface of the snow, we were able to walk easily atop it. We took this opportunity to do some off-road hiking to the north along the power line, an area we'd been unable to reach since the deep snow arrived.

It was easy going, and the air, which warmed quickly, was full of birds. An assorted group of blackbirds—actually a mixed flock of grackles and cowbirds newly arrived from the south—greeted us with their raucous calls. Other birds, juncos from the look of them, twittered overhead as we passed.

At the power line right-of-way, moose tracks meandered through the brushy undergrowth, and we could see where he'd nipped off the buds at the end of many branches.

Still no deer tracks, I thought. Still no gurgling sound of water running in the Elbow Creek. The small changes we were seeing—the shoots of hope that spring was putting out—were still tentative and fragile. Bigger ones were coming, but it would take patience. This was not yet the time.

As we neared the creek, the sun's warm rays had started to soften the snow. One leg went through the crust, and I dropped into snow over my knee.

"Time to get back," I called to Patti, who was exploring up ahead. "Pretty soon, the snow won't support us."

"Okay, but come over here and see this. I think they're pussy willows," she said, enthusiastically pointing.

I got two steps closer, then fell through again. It was time to turn around. "I'll look next time. Right now, we better get into the woods where the sun hasn't weakened the crust."

In the woods, where the trees had shaded the snow, the walking was still good if we stayed away from the tree trunks. Somehow, near the trunks, the snow was softer, and I fell through again.

At the edge of an opening and all the way across the yard, the going was hard, as we both fell through and took turns breaking trail in the hip deep snow.

"We may think it's almost spring," I said between gasping breaths, "but it's still winter out there in the woods."

My legs felt like rubber when we arrived at the driveway and stood puffing until we began to recover. The deep snow was still punishing, and both Patti and I were exhausted by the effort it took to cover a hundred yards.

As the snow disappears, summer birds begin to arrive. Here a goldfinch sits on the deck rail.

❄ New Arrivals ❄

The freezing and thawing continued, and we took early morning walks each day, making certain to start back before the sun had time to weaken the surface. These little "voyages of discovery" took us through the woods in all directions.

One day as we returned along the creek, I stopped at the sound of something odd and held up my hand for Patti to do the same. It was the sound of water running through a hole in the ice. What a crisp, delicious melody.

The next morning, we could hear it from the back deck, a faint but tuneful gurgling in the cool silence.

The April seesaw of seasons was still a standoff, but then came two days of warm sunshine followed by a surprising night rain, first of the year, and the tide started turning. Elbow Creek quit gurgling and started running beneath the ice. With more water coming down from the many square miles of swamp that fed it, the river pressed hard against the bonds that controlled it and piece by piece, the icy restraints let go.

That morning, as I lay in bed, I could hear it, really hear it. There was, from place to place, still ice trying to slow the flow, but the water ran over and around these remnants and pushed them aside.

On our driveway, the slush froze and melted until now it was dirt, sometimes soft, sometimes frozen. In the afternoon, I stood outside clearing a path for melt water to flow across the driveway and disappear beneath a snow bank on the lower side.

That night, with Elbow Creek rumbling in our heads, we were awakened, not gently, by a screaming from outside and pack of cats fleeing from our bed. We both found ourselves already sitting up, wondering what screaming banshee was on our roof.

I got a look up from the window and there, standing on hind legs like a weathervane on the ridgeline of the roof, silhouetted by moonlight, was a furry figure, looking this way and that, apparently frantic.

"What is it?" Patti asked.

"I think it's a raccoon, and he can't get down," I said. "He's hysterical. Keeps trying to start down, but it's too steep. Oops, now there's another one, down below. Oh, no, don't start climbing." I tapped the frosted glass sharply in hopes it would distract him. For now, at least, he stayed on the deck rail with a forepaw on the bottom of the steep A-frame roof.

His friend up above was unable to steel himself for the steep descent, pacing and turning and crying and screaming, but nobody could help.

I was tired, but I was just about to get a ladder and chase him off the roof. The racket was awful, and the cats had all taken cover. Patti said it sounded like he was being murdered.

"Okay, let me see what I can do," I said.

I went to get dressed but before I got even one leg in my pair of pants, there was the unmistakeable sound of claws scratching on the roof above.

"I think he's gonna try it," I said. "He might actually come down."

I went back to the window and watched the frightened raccoon slide down the roof and amazingly jump to the rail where his friend awaited. They looked like two of the three young raccoons who had visited in the fall.

As I watched, I saw that the small raccoon who had stayed below had only a single front leg. It was the smaller of the two raccoons, and the more adventurous young male came over to see if she was all right after he came down from his harrowing perch.

Apparently, the young female had been caught in some kind of trap meant to take a mink or marten at the water's edge. It is said that a trapped raccoon will chew its own leg off to gain freedom, and perhaps that is what happened. As for the third young coon, almost anything might have happened.

The two young raccoons were back a number of times as the water waned, and we got a much better look at them as they sat on the lighted back deck eating sunflower seeds. She did well, the only thing we noticed was that she could not climb a tree.

As I watched, I noted a hint of dawn in the northeast. The clock showed it was just before 5:00 A.M. I hadn't been up so early in a while, and it surprised me. The days were indeed growing longer at a rapid pace, and if I had been a steelhead trout fisherman, I'd be down on the Brule or Cascade or Caribou rivers by now because the word around town was that the fish were beginning their spawning runs from Lake Superior.

Hah, I thought. *You won't catch me out wading those rivers. With snow from horizon to horizon, it's still winter.* I crawled back under the down comforter and, lulled by the tumbling waters of Elbow Creek, went to sleep.

*　*　*

With the creek open and building in volume, the ducks were soon to arrive. A pair of mallards came first; we looked out and there they were, sitting on a rock at the edge of the stream, staring at the water moving by.

Seeing them, we were quick to put a couple of pails full of corn out on a bare spot on the lawn. The inviting brown spot was about six feet in diameter, but to get there I had to trudge through thigh-deep wet snow.

The ducks appear to spend most of their lives staring at the water, but despite this seeming uncomplicated existence, they are not dumb. They knew what we were doing and soon waddled across the snow to reach the food. Then a small flock of mallards dipped low overhead and a half dozen came tumbling out of the sky to make beak-assisted kamikaze landings in the snow.

After a snack, the newcomers settled down with the homesteaders to sit by the creek and stare at the water. We thought no more about the ducks until Patti looked out the kitchen window and said, "Oh, oh," loud enough to alert me to an impending problem.

"What's happening?" I asked.

"Trouble brewing," she replied. "The wood ducks have arrived."

A pair of mallards in early spring.

I smiled at the news, recalling how funny the epic duck battles had been in the fall, and picturing what was about to happen. This was something to see for myself, so I hopped up from the easy chair and hurried to the kitchen window. And there in a small cluster just fifty feet downstream from the mallards, were seven wood ducks—five drakes and two hens.

The wood ducks could have just behaved themselves by sitting quietly and staring at the water, but of course that would have made it too easy. Almost immediately, the two hens, bolder than the colorful but wimpy males, set off for the corn pile. They hadn't gone ten feet when a seemingly half-asleep mallard quit studying the water and slowly turned its head to follow the movement of the stiff-legged wood ducks.

As soon as the mallards realized that their private corn pile was about to be violated, they came to full alert and began to move. And three of them moved fast, cutting off the smaller wood ducks before they could reach the corn.

The woodies did the unexpected. They split and circled the mallards in both directions. One mallard went after one of the wood ducks, but the other two mallards stood watching as the second wood duck looped around them to reach the corn.

Seeing one duck already eating, the big mallard chasing the second duck lost heart and stopped. Now there were two wood ducks at the corn.

Seeing the females eating gave courage to the brilliantly colored drakes. Instead of hiking overland, however, two of them flew straight over the confused mallards and landed in the brown grass. Another followed a few seconds later, landing and skidding forward. Watching from the window, it was impossible not to grin and even laugh out loud at the keystone-cops antics of these ducks. Within minutes, the territorial tide shifted once again as the rest of the mallards came trotting to the attack and scattered the much smaller wood ducks.

I think it went on all day, since each time we looked, the ducks were lined up in new positions as if they were set pieces in a giant chess game. Then finally, bored or full of corn or just plain exhausted, they returned to their original positions along the creek.

For several days, as the creek filled with snow melt, we were treated to regular replays of the duck wars. Sometimes, we would see a hen mallard, followed by a drake, set off into the woods for an exploration. We supposed they were looking for a good place to nest.

One of these hikes led the hen around the house and onto the driveway. A few minutes later, Patti looked out and saw a disturbance and flapping of wings in the dirt. At first she couldn't tell what it was, so she called to me to look outside. By the time I got up and went to the window, she recognized what was going on.

Seeing the duck, a large hawk, probably a red-tailed or red-shouldered hawk, had dropped down to grab her. But the duck was much too large to be carried off. So the hawk held on and flapped his wings while she hunkered down.

By the time I saw the hawk, Patti was racing for the door. Outdoors, the duck had somehow gotten loose and was running for the heavy brush with the flapping hawk in pursuit.

Patti's yell disrupted the life-and-death struggle and caused the hawk to fly up to an overhanging branch, where he perched with a frustrated glare.

"Go! Get away!" She shouted as the door slammed behind her. This sent the hawk flying along with the drake mallard who had been following the hen.

Patti reached the scene of the struggle and found a single drop of blood where the duck had hopped into the crusted snow. There were no prints in the snow and no sign of the hen. Somehow, she had been able to fly away, although it's possible she simply went back to the creek where her friends continued to bob in the eddies or to perch on rocks at the water's edge.

"Where are these hawks coming from?" I asked Patti when she returned. "First those hawks that Bertha teased, and now this one. Seems strange."

She nodded her head, and I could see she was shaking after racing to save the duck.

"I thought for sure the poor duck was gonna be killed," she said with a sigh. "Thank God she got loose."

We wondered where these hawks were coming from because it seemed too early for them to have returned for the summer. Then a couple of days later, as we were driving up a road three miles east of us, we came over a rise and there, staring at us from the center of the gravel, was a huge, mature bald eagle standing over a small pile of fur. Whether he made the kill or found it, we had no way of knowing, but he lifted off without it and flew through the poplars.

We thought about this later; if eagles were here, shouldn't there also be hawks? But we had no answer. Perhaps these were still birds from farther north who were enjoying happy hunting in our more moderate climate and who would be winging north again in a few weeks. We had not seen or heard of the northern owls for a month or more, but we had no way to identify the source of these hunters.

✳ ✳ ✳

Each day I came down the driveway, I could see it literally emerging from the melting snow. I knew there would be plenty of space in which to move snow around. Perhaps it would simply melt on its own without needing to be plowed.

Since daylight savings time had begun, it was light until 7:00 P.M. and definitely leading toward that time when winter turns directly into summer. There is no spring as most know it up here, because when the snow and ice melt, the leaves pop, school ends, and summer begins, all in a matter of days.

Eagle in a dead tree near Greenwood Lake.

That time was still a few weeks away, but we felt it was coming fast. Along the south-facing hill where the snow had melted, crocuses had sprouted, fragile little things that drew strength from the ever-warming sun.

One day, seeing that the snow was retreating across the garden plot, I called Dick Gilbertson to ask about gardening.

"Have you ordered your seeds yet?" He asked.

I replied that I didn't know about ordering seeds.

"Well, you get your seed catalogs in February or March, and then when you decide what to plant, you order the seeds," he explained. "Kind of nice thinking about gardens when it's still cold out."

I told him I'd have to get my seeds downtown at one of the stores, since I had no catalogs and hadn't ordered any garden seed. But I needed to know when to plant.

"We usually figure Memorial Day," he said.

"That late?"

"Well, you don't want 'em to freeze. But sometimes, I'll sneak a few potatoes or other root crops in a few days early if the weather looks good."

"Guess I'm jumping the gun thinking about gardening already," I said with a little embarrassment.

"You can be out tilling, putting weed killer on, fertilizing and so forth earlier in May, but don't go fooling around with those seeds 'til the end of the month."

"I'll take your advice," I said.

❊ ❊ ❊

Despite the fact that snow covered much of the land, I felt the call of the outdoors. With the sun beaming down and April temperatures rising into the mid-forties or even the fifties, I was outdoors under any pretext. I especially enjoyed building drainage ditches to help the runoff cross the drive-way and to cruise about the back roads looking for signs of life.

Patti was more practical. "Let's clean the garage now so we won't have to be out there in a month when everybody else is fishing."

"Fishing, hah!" I said. "The boat is still frozen beneath three feet of snow."

"It won't be long," she warned. "Better get those 'chores' done now."

It was a beautiful day, warming rapidly, and I had a severe case of spring fever. The sun would warm the house in the afternoon and evening without the chip burner, so I shut off the chip feeder to let the fire go out. We decided to make a run to town and then drive along Lake Superior to see how the rivers were running. Anything to avoid cleaning the garage.

Either we could wait for the burner to go out naturally when the chips inside were burned up, or I could save an hour and put it out with a fire extinguisher. At least it seemed a logical though untried solution. I had the big ten-pound extinguisher handy, and I thought this would be the perfect time to test it.

So I descended into the basement of the garage, where I noticed the sump pump was working for the first time, opened the door of the little furnace, and extinguished the fire.

Just as I was thinking how easy it was to put out, the fire reignited with a roar, apparently from its own heat. I gave it another "whoosh" from the extinguisher, this time holding it on a bit longer. The fire went out but reignited with another frightening noise. Each time I put it out, it started again, until the entire ten pounds of retardant had been used. I was amazed and a bit shaken, knowing it was impossible to put out this furnace. We'd have to wait until the unit went out naturally, about forty-five minutes or an hour, before we dared to go.

With the delay, I was shamed into going to work cleaning the garage. The river inspection trip could wait a day.

Bertha accompanied me as I emptied out the garage and burned the accumulated trash. It took about three hours, and, when finished, the place would actually accommodate two cars.

The clouds rolled over us that afternoon, pushed by a strong east wind that built steadily. As I prepared to go inside, Bertha ran ahead and climbed the siding near the front door, then disappeared into a crevice under the eave. I couldn't figure out what she was up to, but as I got inside the family room, I could hear her scratching around inside the wall. Probably found a warm, safe place, I thought, mentioning it to Patti.

In the morning, the cold, hard east wind was carrying snow that had already covered up the promise of spring, once again. We dressed warmly for the blustery weather and set off for a look at the fishing activity on a couple of rivers, the Devil's Track and Cascade.

Along the Lake Superior shoreline, the wind was shrieking and moaning through the trees as ten foot waves assaulted the rocky coast. We went to the two rivers and back home. It was a bitter day, better spent pondering the crackling blaze in the big stone fireplace—a lot like the ducks studying the water.

Such days seem to bring more birds to the feeders, and they puff up to maintain warmth as they eat the seeds. Every two or three days new

A gray jay, a surprisingly uncommon visitor on our deck considering its reputation.

species of birds arrived in this changing season, and we kept our field guides handy on the coffee table. Within the past ten days, we had hosted many siskens, purple finches, and pine grosbeaks, as well as juncos. Brewer's blackbirds, cowbirds, a pair of rose-breasted grosbeaks, several grackles, a gray jay, buntings, and even a few sparrows of unknown variation. The gray jay was an unusual visitor, for despite his well-earned reputation as friend of the woodsman and logger, the gray did not come regularly to our feeders. Of course, our winter regulars—chickadees, blue jays, nuthatches, downy and hairy woodpeckers—all still came, so the railing of the back deck was a busy place.

That evening, on the Duluth TV news, we saw results of the powerful east wind. Driving everything in its path, the wind had blown all the ice still remaining on Lake Superior to the west end of the lake, where it packed together into a massive ice field that stretched twenty miles out from

Storm at Grand Marais.

Duluth and was said to be from three to six feet thick. Shipping was halted and a big ice breaker, probably the *Mackinaw*, was on its way to open a path through the field.

Later, as we watched the national news, we noticed that Bertha's activities in the wall had attracted the notice of our cat Einstein, who had jumped up onto the shelf and was listening attentively to the sounds. We had no idea what she was up to in there; we only hoped she wouldn't emerge inside the house where she would be face to face with the four cats.

The shepherd sisters at play.

18

❆ The Shepherd Sisters ❆

That Sunday morning, we picked up the Duluth paper, and Patti decided to look in the classified ads to see what puppies might be available. We had been talking about dogs in general and how we were always going to be "dog people." I think the unspoken message was that when we saw something interesting, we'd get our next puppy.

"Hmmmm," she said. "This is interesting. A breeder in Wisconsin has two litters of purebred German shepherds."

"Really? I've always wanted one." I replied with interest. "That would be a good dog to have here."

She wrote down the phone number, and, before I realized what was happening, she was talking with the breeder.

"Here," she said, handing me the phone. "Ask him for directions."

The man was near Barron, Wisconsin, about two hundred miles away, and lived on a farm where he bred cattle and dogs. After I wrote a set of complicated directions, I thanked him and hung up.

"Are we ready for this?" I asked. Patti told me what she'd asked him, and we agreed that it was as good a time as any, since these were certainly dogs with excellent bloodlines.

So at 9:30 A.M. on a Sunday morning, we set off for central Wisconsin. As we neared Duluth, we got to see for ourselves the massive ice field, with an icebreaker leading a pair of ships through it toward safe harbor.

"That stuff is not gonna melt anytime soon," I said, showing a terrific grasp of the obvious.

Patti rolled her eyes and responded in kind, "Right, Sherlock," she said.

We drove another two hours and finally arrived at a very elegant and prosperous looking farm with a huge house.

We followed the dogman to the back of the house, where he loosed about twenty puppies. They were tagged with blue and red ribbon collars and had been pre-selected for quality. When that many puppies tumbled and jumped around, trying to get a good look at them is virtually impossible.

Patti sat on the floor, and, suddenly, one female puppy jumped into her lap and began licking her hand.

"I like this one," she said.

"Great," said the dog man, "Well, that was easy."

"We're not done," I said suddenly. "I think we need two females." Patti and I had talked about this and decided that two dogs would be workable and would also provide each other with a playmate and companion.

"The one you've picked is from a German blood line. Very dominant. If you want two, the second one needs to be more submissive."

We worked through about three pups until finding one that he thought would work. This one was from American bloodlines, different parents.

Half an hour later, we drove away with two ten-week-old shepherd puppies that were anything but docile. We had brought a box along to put them in on the way home; they were out of that within a couple of miles.

Patti played with the beautiful pups, and we thought of dog names. The German dog would be Sheba, the American dog Shadow.

Things went well until we reached the outskirts of Grand Marais. After four hours in the car, everything let loose—one pooped while the other threw up. Then they romped through the mess and spread it around. Groaning at the dual disaster, I pulled up next to the old court house, and we literally shoveled out the mess; it was everywhere. Six miles from home; they could have done everything there.

The smell in the Jeep was enough to gag us both, so we started up the hill and ultimately drove all the way to the house with the windows half open and the cold air blasting us.

"I'm freezing," I said.

"Tough," Patti replied, "If I roll up the windows and the smell comes back, I'll throw up too."

This episode later became one of the funniest stories we ever experienced, but, at the moment, it was horrific. The two puppies were happily tracking through what was left of the mess, then climbing into our laps. There was no escape.

Finally, we pulled up before the garage and removed the puppies from the car. Despite the fact these two pups had never been outdoors before, they happily found a snow bank to lie in while chewing the snow. We went in, carefully pulled off all our outerwear and washed up before starting fresh on the car.

Ultimately, Patti handled the car while I found fifty feet of snow fencing and made a pen between the garage and house. The two puppies, whom we had already started calling the Shepherd Sisters even though they weren't actually sisters, felt right at home in the deep snow and romped in loops around their new outdoor playground.

Indoors, however, it was a story of too much, too fast for our cats, who fled in terror to their upstairs sanctuary. The puppies were already too big and aggressive for the cats, and that disparity would only become more pronounced as the shepherds grew. We had somehow miscalculated this relationship. For now, at least, we would give the dogs a run of the basement and first floor during the day, and set up a comfortable sleeping area in the basement at night. The cats would stay upstairs all day, then have both that floor and first floor at night, when they liked to roam. This worked so well that we made it a permanent arrangement.

The two rowdy puppies signaled a rebirth of sorts that provided a cue for the weather to follow. Sunny days in the fifties soon brought the mountainous snow banks down to knee-high size and drove the snow back into the shadows. One morning I looked and the yard was partially snowless, though still brown.

And then, in the space of a day, two things happened that left us with big smiles. The first surprise came in the morning as we took the pups for a walk down the driveway. Overhead was the familiar gravel voice of our friend, Poe the raven. We had been seeing him and his mate, but never together on a regular basis, and we surmised they were taking turns sitting a nest.

But now, along with Poe, a second shadow passed over and then a third. We looked up at the blue sky and there they were, Poe, his mate, and their baby, who was almost as large as his parents. What a wonder.

Patti ran back to the house for some scraps to set out in honor of the occasion, and the trio landed overhead. This

The first flowers pop out as the snow leaves.

time Poe and his mate waited until we nearly rounded the corner before dropping down while Poe Junior sat above.

When we came back, the ravens and scraps were gone, but the trio made regular appearances after that. They even sat on the shed and talked to us as we tilled the garden and picked rocks.

And then that evening, the deer came back. There were five of them that visited the corn pile, a large doe and her two yearling fawns, an apparently pregnant smaller doe, and another small deer of unknown sex or age. They were gaunt and hungry after a long, hard winter and a bit jittery at their surroundings, as if they expected a wolf to come sliding out of the darkness at any moment. The old doe was as bossy as ever, demanding that her kids eat first before the others, but their re-appearance was a welcome sight.

When it was almost dark, we stopped watching and went into the family room, where two of the cats took up position for a vigil at the wall where Bertha had gone several days

Poe, the Raven, and his family.

earlier. Inside the wall, there was a lot of scratching, and we wondered if perhaps there was more than just one squirrel in there.

For a couple of days, as the sun shone down and the snow melted, we enjoyed all the new activity around the house. Deer, ducks, ravens, and huge flocks of migrating birds all entertained from dawn 'til dusk, when we weren't already busy with two supercharged puppies whose ears still flopped around instead of standing erect. It was a wonderful time, and we eagerly scanned the treetops for any catkins and tell-tale signs of buds we might see, but they remained reddish in color. Still too early, we were told.

Doe checking to see if it's okay to come out of the woods.

19

❄ New Life ❄

On the last Saturday of the month, as I sat down on the front steps to take in the rapidly changing scene. I was joined briefly by Bertha, who came down the wall and ran over to look in the garage, then returned.

"Well, old girl, what are you up to in there?" I asked, thinking that it looked like a secure place to have a house.

She chirped twice, then climbed back up the rough-sawn cedar siding and disappeared into the narrow opening. But she wasn't gone for more than twenty seconds before reappearing, then turning toward the opening where a second squirrel's head appeared. Then out came a perfect little squirrel, about three fourths as large as Bertha.

Gently holding the baby in her mouth, she lowered herself down the siding and ran past me to the garage. How she could hold the baby as she ran was anyone's guess, but she did. In the garage, she climbed onto the work bench and deposited the baby in one of the two snowmobile helmets sitting on the counter.

As she returned to her nest inside the wall of the house, I called Patti to come and see this amazing show. We sat quietly on the wooden walkway as she

hauled baby number two into the garage, then returned
for a third.

"Isn't this amazing?" I asked in a whisper.

"Awesome," Patti replied quietly. "I can't believe
how large those babies are. How can she carry them?"

I shrugged, equally mystified, as we watched Bertha
carry five young squirrels, one after another, and
deposit them in the two snowmobile helmets on the
bench.

After the work was completed, she came and laid at
our side like a winded dog, and Patti gave her an
almond to munch.

But the peace was soon disrupted by a clatter in the
garage, where the babies had successfully escaped and
sent one of the helmets tumbling. Bertha raced to the
rescue as we peeked in to see squirrels scampering

Patti and Bertha.

back and forth across the work surface looking for a way to escape.

She got them under control long enough to lead them across a board and up a narrow passageway to the upstairs level, which was where we guessed she had planned to take them all along.

Once in the safety of the upstairs storage area, there were all sorts of interesting places to explore. We could hear the activity as we backed away.

Outside, the quiet was interrupted by a sound from above.

Overhead, soaring on the wind, were three majestic ravens, Poe and his family. The sight, combined with Bertha's miracle, was enough to make us stop and hold each other's hand.

When Patti spoke, she had tears in her eyes. "This is so wonderful, to be here and see this rebirth going on all around us. I can certainly take the winter if it will always end like this."

I nodded and pulled her close, and we stood holding each other, not speaking because no words were necessary.

Looking around, I realized that finally, it was true. Our winter had almost ended. The lawn, in all the places the sun could reach, was free of snow. The frost was coming up out of the ground. There was new life all around for us to enjoy. Even the aluminum hull of our fishing boat was visible behind the garage.

In the next few days, we watched Bertha teach her brood the basics. Knowing nothing, it took some time for them to learn that seeds were good to eat and German shepherd puppies were not to be played with. But Bertha got them successfully through the hoops, and when I looked upstairs in the garage for some life preservers, all five were still scampering happily.

We made a repeat trip to the mouth of the Devil's Track and Cascade rivers on a sunny day and found the fishermen clamoring over rocks and across the remaining snow banks in search of steelhead trout. While we were watching from the bridge, we heard the haunting, unmistakeable call of a loon some distance out on Lake Superior. Later that day, I mentioned the loon and was told that they are always back around May 1st, but stayed on Lake Superior until the ice went out on the inland lakes where they nest and raise their young.

That afternoon, we were greeted by our old chipmunk friend Chester, who had apparently found a way out through the snow bank that still covered his hole. With half a tail, he was easy to identify.

"Chester," Patti called. "Where'd you come from? Are you hungry for a nut?"

Naturally, Chester took that as an invitation, and was soon climbing her pant leg to reach the table top, where he filled his cheeks with almonds.

"I wonder if he finally ran out of food or if it was simply time to come out," I said. "Seems like the whole world's coming alive these days."

"Now all we need is for the ice to go off the lakes, and we'll be able to bid winter goodbye," Patti added.

I nodded. Just two days earlier, we'd driven three miles up the Gunflint Trail to the gravel road that led to Elbow Lake landing. Other than a snow bank the plows had piled earlier in the winter, the road was navigable with our four by four. At the end of the road, corrugated gray ice still lay across the lake, but it was rotting in the sun and had pulled away from the shore at least ten feet. I knew it wouldn't be long until the ice vanished. A good breeze would do it.

Knowing that spring and summer were just around the corner didn't make it happen. Winter does not give up easily in the north country. That night on TV, they predicted a storm. Might be rain, might be snow, might be something in between, but something was coming.

The morning dawned cold and cloudy with a chill, damp wind blowing. More likely to be snow than rain, the weatherman said. By noon, snow slanted across the sky, sticking to the grass, deflating our dreams of tulips and tree buds. It came down hard and heavy, reducing visibility. It was even covering the road and turning the blacktop to ice.

I sat in my upstairs office, trying to write but unable to focus on anything but the suddenly white world.

When we went down the driveway with the pups to fetch the mail, the school bus was already lumbering by, heading north. The mail box was still empty. They let school out early, I thought, and the mailman's late. Must be bad weather everywhere.

It was bad, and then it got worse. South of us a mile or so was an opening on the Gunflint Trail where the wind blew freely. In that area, a drift had formed that now blocked the road. We got this news at suppertime from a neighbor down the road, who had just been outside, trying fruitlessly to extricate a car from the drift.

"Where are the plows?" I asked.

"Everybody took their plows off," he said. "The county trucks are hauling sand and gravel. They figured the snow season, at least the serious snow season, was over. I don't know what they plan to do. Maybe nothing. After all, how long can this last?"

I had no answer for that question, because in intensity, this surprise May storm matched anything we'd seen all winter. We had stopped using the basement furnace and were heating with electrically warmed water when necessary. I cranked up the fireplace to add

Scenes from the ice storm.

more heating power. It felt good and took off the chill as the wind moaned outside.

"May sixth and we get the worst storm of the season," I fretted. "How can this be happening?" Patti was about to answer when a crack of lightning lit the snow-filled sky and was followed by a shattering ka-boom.

"Must be what they call 'thundersnow,'" I said in amazement. "This is another first for me."

At some point in the night, I awoke to hear ice pelting our bedroom windows. By morning, we had about five inches of ice-encrusted snow. It looked once again like mid-winter.

But this time, the cold ended quickly as the clouds broke up and the warm sunshine melted the ice. In two days, remnants of the storm had vanished, and when our grass emerged, we saw a definite green hue to it. Birds seemed to be everywhere, singing the songs that had been silent when the snow returned.

We sat outside at the wrought iron table and shared our sandwiches with Bertha, Chester, and two or three of their more courageous cousins and kids. Down by the creek, which was now ice-free and running hard from the extra snow melt, a few ducks still hunkered down on rocks or paddled in the quiet eddies.

That afternoon, a breeze piped up and blew the ice out of several nearby lakes, including our choice for the fishing opener on the coming weekend, Elbow Lake. I was out in the garage unloading Orange Julius and restoring the trailer to its original function as a hauler of boats.

The fishing opener is the official start of spring or whatever that season is that bridges winter and high summer for a couple of short weeks. Suddenly there are boats on trailers around town, bigger boats than any of the locals use. Minnows are in demand again by eager anglers, and half a dozen shoppers can be found examining the tackle display at Buck's hardware or over at

Butch Schulte's station. The weather might be too cold to fish or at least too cold for the fish to bite, but there was always that wonderful anticipation that any change of season brings in Minnesota.

So I got the trailer ready and dislodged the four-teen-foot aluminum boat from its own personal snow-drift on the north side of the garage and loaded it on the trailer. Then came the motor, our trusty old ten-horse Johnson, the anchor, oars, and other necessities.

They say a motor should be "winterized" by drain-ing it of gas and installing fresh plugs. This particular Johnson was already nearing thirty years of age and sufficed well enough to always start on the second pull without any of the recommended maintenance.

With the boat, motor, and accoutrements loaded on the trailer, I called Patti outside for a presentation. "Ta da," I said with a flourish.

She smiled and toured the boat, then walked away saying, "It's not quite ready."

"What do you mean?" I asked, disappointed.

"Isn't there supposed to be a plug in the bottom?" She asked, arching eyebrows in that sassy way.

I looked near the stern, and there indeed was a hole in the bottom where the plug should have been. Chagrined, I thought about where I might have put it way back seven months previous in October. I wandered into the garage, deep in thought and worry. Surely I'd put it somewhere special so it couldn't get lost, but where?

I looked in all the likely spots. Then I looked in all the likely spots again. No plug.

The door opened. Patti peeked out. "Find it yet?"

I shook my head no.

She grinned. "Go look in the center console of the Jeep. I think that's the place you've been putting stuff that absolutely, positively can't be lost."

Henrietta, the groundhog, exiting the feed box.

A hopeful look erased my fears as I leaned in and opened the console. Outboard motor shear pins. Snowmobile keys. Insurance card. Boat plug. Bingo! End of problem.

"Whew!" I said out loud. "I doubt if there's another one just like this in a hundred miles. The boat's thirty years old. Not so many like it around anymore and that's one problem I couldn't fix with duct tape. Probably would have needed one of those wooden plugs, and that would have leaked like a sieve."

I screwed the plug into the hole and relaxed. We were ready. A run downtown for minnows packed in oxygen, and we were set to get up in the morning, run the pups, and go fishing.

We got up at 5:30 A.M., and it was already bright daylight, though the sun was obscured behind a film of pink and gold clouds in the east. By six, we were loaded and rolling toward the lake. It looked like a nice day, with a high in the fifties.

The boat slid into the water, and the Johnson came to life after a long, frozen winter. We were the only car in the parking lot, and soon our boat motored out of sight around the "elbow" in the lake. We continued toward a place we'd discovered in the fall near the far end of the lake where Elbow Creek ran out of the lake on its journey to our house.

As we skimmed along, hunkered down against the cool wind, the wooded hills passed alongside. Here and there we could see large patches of snow, where winter still held its grip.

I slowed the motor and tried to remember the exact position from last fall, but it was difficult. How soon we forget even important things. Finally, I slipped the anchor overboard, and we drifted to the end of the rope.

A few casts later, we had a bite. At least we were in the right place, I thought. And then I hooked a nice walleye and brought it aboard.

"Only one more and we'll have dinner," I said.

We settled to wait, enjoying the beauty of the land, its blue water and rolling hills.

Just then, a cracking branch caused us to focus on the shoreline not more than fifty yards away. A large, dark shape moved through the brush and revealed itself as a moose. Besides her was a fawn-colored calf, still slightly wobbly on its long, spindly legs.

The cow moved to the water's edge and drank. The little calf stayed close, almost touching his mother as she moved. We were downwind and sat silently watching, so she didn't notice us.

The cow nipped at buds as the calf nursed, and we watched the miracle of new life. Time passed as they worked their way along the shore and the sun came out.

Finally, Patti's line went taut, and she set the hook on a second walleye. As she landed the fish, it flopped noisily against the metal boat and alerted the cow to our presence. In two steps, she melted into the branches and was gone, with her calf alongside like a light tan shadow.

We got the walleye under control and talked about the incredible pleasure and privilege of watching the cow and calf for so long.

"Must have been a half hour," I suggested.

"And walleyes for supper as a bonus," Patti exclaimed. Her love of fishing knew no bounds.

"Wait, listen," I said, thinking I'd just heard a song I recognized. We waited silently, then we both heard it, the song of the white-throated sparrow, a sure sign of spring and, by our standards, the prettiest song to be heard in the northern woods.

Goosebumps rose suddenly on my arms. That's what the song of the white-throated sparrow did to me.

I pulled in the anchor and started the motor. We'd caught our fish and had our thrills. Time to go home. And then I looked again at the hillside to the southwest, where the aspens and birches stood tall.

"Take a look back on the hillside and tell me what color you see," I said, pointing.

"It's green," she said. "The lightest, palest green I've ever seen, but it's green."

It was true. The birch buds were opening and the catkins forming on the aspens. After seven months, the cycle of new life was abroad in the north country and winter was over.

❄ Postscript ❄

After fifteen years in Florida, the winter of 1988-1989 seemed quite severe, but it was not particularly noteworthy as northeastern Minnesota winters go.

Heavy snow early, light snow late in the winter, and normal temperatures. There have been earlier winters, later springs, heavier snowfalls and open winters; the variety is never ending, and we saw much different conditions in subsequent years.

One year, winter came to stay on Halloween as three feet of snow fell. There was no frost in the ground and root crops left out over the winter were still edible in the spring.

Another winter, the snow was virtually gone in mid-April, allowing travel on the back roads all through the spring.

The winter of 1995-1996 was the hardest ever. For five consecutive mornings in early February, we recorded temperatures of -41, -41, -43, -34, and -41.

That spring, ice still covered all county lakes on the opening day of fishing season. Many anglers walked out on the ice and drilled holes to ice fish that day. The leaves did not start to bud until Memorial Day, when there was still snow in the woods.

About the Author

Jack Becklund was born and raised in Minnesota. He is the author of two previous books, *Summers with the Bears* (Hyperion 1999) and *Golden Fleece* (St. Martin 1990). After a career in advertising and publishing, he and his wife, Patti, are retired and reside in Alabama.